The geomorphology
of the British Isles

General editors:
Eric H Brown and Keith Clayton

Scotland

In the same series

Northern England   *Cuchlaine A M King*

In preparation

Wales and Southwest England
Eric H Brown, D Q Bowen & R S Waters

Southeast and Southern England   *D K C Jones*

Midlands and Eastern England
Keith Clayton & Allan Straw

Ireland   *G L Davies & N Stephens*

Scotland

J B Sissons

Methuen & Co Ltd

QE 264
S 56

First published in 1976 by
Methuen & Co Ltd, 11 New Fetter Lane, London EC4P 4EE

©1976 J.B. Sissons

Printed in Great Britain by Butler & Tanner Ltd. Frome & London

ISBN 0 416 83990 8 (hardbound edition)
ISBN 0 416 84000 0 (paperback edition)

This title is available in both hardbound and paperback editions. The
paperback edition is sold subject to the condition that it shall not, by way
of trade or otherwise, be lent, resold, hired out or otherwise circulated
without the publisher's prior consent in any form of binding or cover
other than that in which it is published and without a similar condition
including this condition being imposed on the subsequent purchaser.

Distributed in the USA by
Harper & Row Publishers Inc. Barnes & Noble Import Division

Contents

Continued

General Editors' Preface

The British Isles is a most varied and complex part of the world, and over a long period it has been studied in great detail by geologists and geomorphologists. Several general studies of the geology and scenery type have appeared, but despite the wealth of the published literature, more detailed work has been limited to a few regions. Indeed, although the most ambitious work, Wooldridge and Linton on Southeast England was first published in 1938, no comparable volume has covered any other part of England.

The main difficulty facing anyone writing about the landforms of the British Isles and their history is the paradox that despite a very considerable literature, the gaps and uncertainties seem to diminish very little over the years. It is often said that each piece of research exposes half a dozen new problems, and so far most of the published literature has tended to add to the complexity of our knowledge. The only way out of this problem is through the establishment of more general concepts into which this detail will fit, and this is the role of this series of books on the different parts of the British Isles. The synthesis is certainly not easy, and it is obviously incomplete. Our understanding of the present land surface and its relationship with the underlying geology (whether 'solid' or 'drift') is relatively secure, but the historical background to the present, complicated as it is by the fluctuating environments of Quaternary time, is less well known. Each author has brought his own special interests and expertise to the synthesis of the region he knows best. To conclude the series, a summary volume by the editors will seek common strands in the regional summaries and erect a national framework within which the more detailed regional accounts will fit.

While no standard approach has been imposed on the contributing authors, care has been taken to be consistent in the use of terminology and in the recently-elaborated Quaternary timescale (Mitchell *et al* 1973) has everywhere been used. Correlation tables are provided for each region, while the maps and diagrams will be found particularly valuable since those in the published literature are so scattered, and generally refer to quite small areas.

Above all these volumes will make the existing literature accessible to those who want to seek more detail on a particular point and will make it digestible to the greater number who seek a wider evolutionary understanding of the landforms of the very diverse regions of the British Isles.

Preface

Scotland contains a great variety of glacial landforms including excellent examples of many types of feature. Fluvioglacial landforms also abound, periglacial forms are widespread on the higher ground, while many parts of the coast have suites of raised marine features. With such an abundance of material for study it is hardly surprising that only limited attention has been paid to the preglacial landforms that evolved during some 70 million years of Tertiary time. In fact no significant contribution in this field has been made for some years, although scores of papers concerned with Quaternary landforms, and particularly with the sequence of Quaternary events, have appeared during the last few years. This book reflects the situation by Quaternary topics constituting seven chapters out of nine.

References cited are intentionally restricted, and preference given particularly in the later chapters to publications that have appeared in the last ten years or so. Partly this is because older literature is considered at some length in the author's earlier book *The evolution of Scotland's scenery*, and partly it reflects a recent rapid increase in geomorphological publications. Despite this increase, there is still remarkably little geomorphological information on large areas of Scotland: for many areas the most detailed material is in Geological Survey memoirs of over half a century ago, and for some parts there is no detailed information at all. Clearly, there is great scope for geomorphological research in Scotland.

The author wishes to express his gratitude to many researchers who have generously provided him with unpublished information. Specific acknowledgements are made in the text.

J.B. Sissons   July, 1974

I   Rocks and relief

The bedrock geology of Scotland is extremely varied and has exerted a profound influence on ground form both on the large and small scale. This has long been recognised but no detailed quantitative studies have been undertaken to show precisely why certain rocks are relatively resistant to erosion (of various types) and why others are relatively weak in this respect. Despite the lack of such data the consideration of Scottish landforms must begin with the relationship between rocks and relief.

Although there are strong morphological contrasts between western and eastern Scotland, the long established three-fold division of the mainland into Highlands, Central Lowlands and Southern Uplands recognises basic morphological and geological differences. The Highlands, along with the Outer Hebrides and the Shetland Islands, are formed mainly of severely folded, meta-morphosed and intruded rocks, although along the northwest coast of the mainland some rocks dating back to pre-Cambrian times have escaped significant modification. Folding was less severe in the Southern Uplands and metamorphism was mainly restricted to the aureoles of the several granite intrusions. All these old rocks form the resistant core of Scotland: they are surrounded and partly covered unconformably by rocks of Old Red and younger ages (fig. 1.1).

Central Lowlands
The Central Lowlands are the principal area developed on these younger rocks. Despite their name their relief is very varied: many hills exceed 300 m and the highest points rise above 600 m. Yet their average altitude is low compared with that of the High-lands or Southern Uplands on either side. A striking feature is the

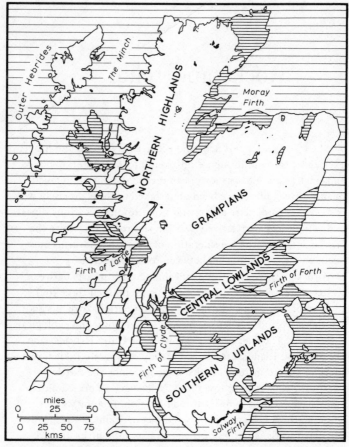

Fig. 1.1   Distribution of cover rocks.

extremely common (though not universal) correspondence of igneous rocks with relatively high ground and sedimentary strata with relatively low ground.

Along the Highland border of the Central Lowlands a belt of low ground extends the whole width of Scotland. It includes Strathmore and the Howe of the Mearns, Strathearn, Strathallan, the Carse of Stirling and the low ground at the southern end of Loch Lomond (fig. 1.2). This lowland strip corresponds with Old

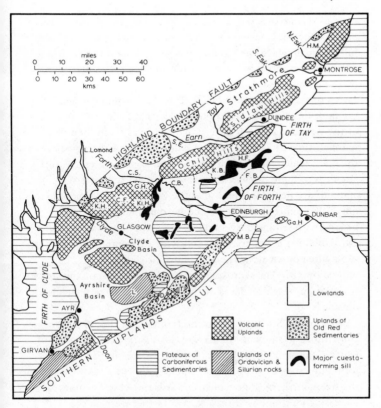

Fig. 1.2   Geology and relief in the Central Lowlands. C.B. Clackmannan basin. C.F. Campsie Fells. C.S. Carse of Stirling. D. Douglas basin. F.B. Fife basin. G.H. Gargunnock Hills. Ga.H. Garleton Hills. H.F. Howe of Fife. H.M. Howe of the Mearns. K.B. Kinross basin. K.H. Kilpatrick Hills. Ki.H. Kilsyth Hills. L. Lesmahagow Hills. M.B. Midlothian basin. S. Strathallan. S.E. Strathearn. T. Tinto Hills.

Red strata that are mainly weak sandstones, shales and marls, although the bedrock itself is usually hidden beneath thick drift deposits. In places along the edge of the Highlands the Old Red strata, especially coarse conglomerates, are much more resistant and are associated with hilly ground that attains its greatest altitude of 665 m in Uamh Bheag (figs. 1.2–1.4).

Southwest of the Old Red lowland a line of lava hills is continuous from coast to coast except for deep narrow gaps at Perth, Stirling, Strathblane and the Clyde estuary. Along with the lava hills through which the Lanarkshire-Ayrshire border runs, these uplands are typified by craggy, often-stepped rock outcrops and by numerous cuestas, although the latter rarely continue far owing to the frequency of faults. The most prominent feature is the fault-line scarp, 500 to 600 m high, that forms the south face of the western Ochils. It is here that the lavas reach their maximum altitude of 720 m, partly a consequence of their great thickness which, along with interbedded agglomerates and tuffs, amounts to 2000 m. Northeastwards through the eastern Ochils and Sidlaws altitudes diminish as the volcanic rocks thin out (to only 200 m in coastal Angus) and become increasingly interbedded with sedimentary strata. The Firth of Tay and adjacent Carse of Gowrie, underlain by Old Red sedimentary strata long ago faulted down along the axis of an anticline and later exploited by differential erosion, are bordered by steep fault-line scarps from which the lavas of the Sidlaws and eastern Ochils dip outwards.

West of the Stirling gap Carboniferous lavas and related rocks constitute a prominent hill mass that has various local names of which Campsie Fells is the best known. Successive lava flows form numerous small steps that can be followed for kilometres on the steep northern slope which, towards the west, becomes an increasingly pronounced feature. Yet farther west, in the Kilpatrick Hills, this feature is absent although the rocks are similar. In part this may reflect the steeper dip of the lavas in the Kilpatrick Hills, but it is probably due essentially to erosion by the powerful Highland ice-stream that flowed down the valley now occupied by Loch Lomond and across the hills.

In the axial tract of the Central Lowlands, where Carboniferous sedimentary rocks are widespread, most of the striking relief features are related to igneous intrusions and extrusions. The sedimentary rocks themselves are mainly associated with subdued forms and gently-undulating ground (although locally they may form distinct features such as the anticlinal ridge lying east of the Midlothian basin). Partly this is due to glacial action, especially the deposition of till, coupled with the infilling of

closed depressions with lake deposits, while peat is extensive in
places. But it primarily reflects the nature of the rocks themselves.
Thus the series of thick sandstone beds that occurs in part of the
English Carboniferous succession, particularly in the Pennines, is
represented in Scotland by a very much diminished sequence.
Similarly, although the word 'limestone' is prominent in the
names given to the divisions of the Scottish Carboniferous, most
of the limestones are only a few metres thick (20 m is
exceptional) and karstic landforms are absent. The Carboniferous
sedimentary rocks are, in fact, characterised by rapid vertical
variations in lithology with few major resistant beds so that
distinctive features are scarce. For the most part the ground
becomes lower towards the central parts of the three main basins
(Midlothian-Fife, Lanarkshire-Clackmannanshire and Ayrshire).
Coal Measure strata often occupy the lowest ground, probably
reflecting the prevalence of weak sandstones and shales.

The junction of the Central Lowlands with the Southern
Uplands is well defined in the east where it is marked almost
everywhere by an abrupt ascent along the line of the Southern
Uplands fault. This linear feature becomes less clear towards the
Clyde, beyond which the fault often corresponds with valleys,
such as Glen App draining into Loch Ryan. Here the fault does
not separate areas of contrasting relief for on its northwestern
side there are extensive uplands with summits typically between
400 and 500 m. This may help to explain why it has become
firmly established in elementary geographical teaching that the
Southern Uplands fault extends from Dunbar to Girvan when in
fact it reaches the coast nearly 30 km southwest of Girvan (fig.
1.2).

Ground that is dominantly hill country extends from the
Pentlands to the Firth of Clyde, but small lowland tracts are
present such as the Douglas basin, which corresponds with a down-
faulted outlier of Carboniferous strata. Relief is strongly affected
by faults parallel with the Southern Uplands fault, the most
important being the Pentlands-Straiton fault, which crosses the
coast at Girvan. Within the faulted belt Ordovician and Silurian
inliers occur. The anticlinal Lesmahagow inlier, associated with
200 km^2 of hill country is the largest (fig. 1.2) and, like the much

smaller Hagshaw Hills anticline, is composed mainly of greywackes and shales. Nearby, Old Red sedimentary and volcanic
rocks correspond with another hilly tract, the former reaching
593 m in Cairn Table (fig. 1.6). Farther northeast the Pentland
Hills constitute a narrow belt of high ground. Near Edinburgh
they are mainly composed of volcanic rocks (fig. 1.3) and tend to
have rather sharp summits, but southwestwards Old Red sandstones and conglomerates dominate and the hills are smoother
in outline.

In addition to the major outcrops of igneous rock mentioned
above, there are innumerable smaller igneous outcrops in the
Central Lowlands, especially in the areas where Carboniferous
strata are at the surface. The associated landforms are often
closely related to the nature of the intrusion or extrusion. Of the
hundreds of volcanic necks that exist nearly all are less than a
kilometre in diameter. Although some of the very small ones,
merely tens of metres across, have little or no effect on relief,
some of the larger ones appear as striking isolated hills, frequently

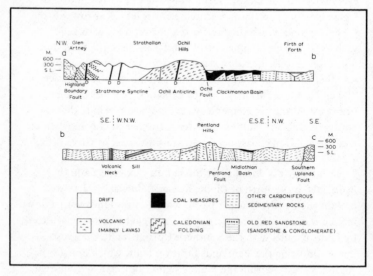

Fig. 1.3   Geological section across the Central Lowlands through the Ochil
and Pentland hills. D. Dyke.

of asymmetrical form owing to glacial action. They include Largo
Law on the northern side of the Firth of Forth; North Berwick
Law on the southern side and, nearby, rising precipitously from
the firth itself, the Bass Rock; Arthur's Seat and the Castle Rock
in Edinburgh; Dumbarton Rock commanding the Clyde estuary;
and Neilston Pad located in one of the gaps leading southwest
from Glasgow (fig. 1.4).

Craggy lava outcrops typify the Garleton Hills in East Lothian,
the Bathgate Hills in West Lothian and the Braid Hills in Edinburgh. In the ground between the river Clyde and the Firth of
Forth straight low rocky ridges mark the outcrops of thick east-
west dykes. Laccolithic intrusions, forming hills with rather
rounded outline, are represented by Black Hill in the Pentlands,
Traprain Law standing isolated in East Lothian, and the Tinto
Hills rising to 712 m from the Clyde valley close to the Southern
Uplands fault. Black Hill and the Tinto Hills are composed of
felsite, which crops out at various other points towards the
Southern Uplands as, for example, in the sills that constitute

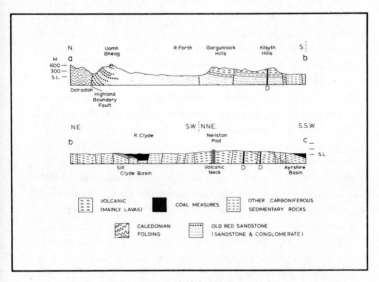

Fig. 1.4   Geological section across the Central Lowlands from Uamh
Bheag to the Ayrshire basin. D. Dyke.

Garleffin Fell and Glenalla Fell in Ayrshire. Many other hills in
the Central Lowlands are associated with sills. They are common
in lowland Ayrshire (e.g. Craigie Hill near Kilmarnock) and are
represented in Edinburgh by Corstorphine Hill and Salisbury
Crags, while the flat-topped Isle of May at the entrance to the
Firth of Forth is an isolated example. The most important sill, up
to 180 m thick, underlies a large area around the Firth of Forth
(fig. 1.2) and its faulted outcrop forms a series of prominent
features. Stirling Castle stands on the summit of one outcrop and
Wallace's monument on another, while on the flanks of the
uplands southwest of Stirling the sill appears as a conspicuous
cuesta. It forms hill country near Torphichen in West Lothian and
corresponds with the constriction in the Firth of Forth utilised
by the Forth bridges. In its most pronounced outcrop it reaches
an altitude of 450 m, its escarpment standing as much as 340 m
above the adjacent Kinross basin.

Southern Uplands

Most of Scotland south of the Southern Uplands fault is hill
country, although important lowland areas occur in the Tweed
basin and finger inland from the shores of the Solway (fig. 1.5).
Much the greater part of the high ground is composed of folded
Ordovician and Silurian sedimentary rocks, mainly greywackes,
shales and mudstones, that are associated with the typical
Southern Uplands scenery of rounded hills and smooth slopes.
These forms relate largely to the rapid lithological variations and
often steep dip that cause individual beds to have narrow outcrops that have not favoured the production of large structurally-
controlled features. Weathering of these rocks rarely results in the
production of boulders but instead produces mainly small flattish
stones and lesser debris that contribute further to the rounded
appearance. Rougher forms do occur, however. For example,
bands of coarse grit and conglomerate form crags and irregular
ridges, as in a belt extending southwest from Queensberry Hill
near the river Nith. Bare rock is also common in and near some of
the highest ground owing to glacial erosion, as in the Tweedsmuir
Hills, but even here Broad Law (839 m), the second highest point
in southern Scotland, has a broad gently-rounded summit.

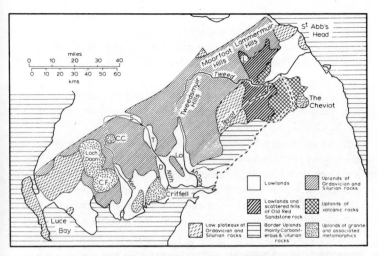

Fig. 1.5   Geology and relief in the Southern Uplands. C.C. Cairnsmore of Carsphairn. C.F. Cairnsmore of Fleet. D. Dumfries basin. L. Lauderdale. Lo. Lochmaben basin. S. Sanquhar basin. T. Thornhill basin.

Valleys in the Ordovician and Silurian rocks are usually narrow, deep and steep-sided. While many of the principal streams flow discordantly to the grain of the rocks, numerous minor streams occupy straight southwest or northeast valleys along the strike. Some valleys follow fault lines, the most notable being the trench containing the Moffat Water.

Parts of the area underlain by Ordovician and Silurian strata are distinguished from the main area in figure 1.5. In the extreme east, inland from St Abb's Head, a pronounced plateau occurs between 200 and 240 m over a considerable area, while on the opposite side of the country an extensive area of subdued relief lies mostly between 150 and 250 m. A glacially-eroded plateau mainly between 300 and 400 m occurs between the rivers Ettrick and Teviot, these streams and the Borthwick Water and Ale Water following ice-modified valleys well below its general level. South-east of the river Teviot the Silurian rocks are interrupted by a number of small igneous intrusions that appear as prominent hills such as Rubers Law. Farther southeast Carboniferous sedimentary rocks crop out. At their base are the Birrenswark lavas,

which appear intermittently over a distance of 70 km parallel
with the Border and form a series of cuestas.

In the western Southern Uplands variety in the relief is provided by granite batholiths. The Criffel and Cairnsmore of Fleet
intrusions form bold massive hills with rounded outlines. Where
strongly affected by glacial erosion the granite terrain may be
extremely irregular, however, as in the less elevated western part
of the Criffel granite outcrop with its numerous rock knobs and
hollows and craggy hills. The Cairnsmore of Carsphairn granite
rises above the surrounding Ordovician rocks to attain 796 m, but
the Loch Doon granite outcrop is largely surrounded by higher
ground corresponding with its metamorphic aureole. A considerable part of the granite basin lies below 300 m, but the metamorphosed Ordovician sediments reach 813 m in the Kells Range
to the east and 842 m in Merrick to the west. The metamorphic
outcrop often corresponds with very rough ground with
numerous bare rock ribs and the scenery resembles that of the
western Highlands. Standing separate from the western granites is
the mass forming the peat-covered dome-like summit of The
Cheviot (816 m). This granite is surrounded by an extensive outcrop of Old Red lavas forming the usual craggy hills dissected by
deep, narrow valleys.

The lower ground of the Tweed basin comprises three morphological units related to geology. The lowest ground, in the east, is
mainly coincident with Carboniferous sedimentary strata largely
concealed beneath thick drift that is strongly drumlinised. To the
southwest a curved belt of low hills corresponds with a faulted
outcrop of Carboniferous lavas. This is succeeded by an area of
Old Red sedimentary rocks, interrupted by a series of intrusions
that form conspicuous hills. Among the latter are the two
Dirrington laws, composed of felsite, Fans Hill formed of
agglomerate, and the Eildon Hills (422 m), of trachyte and felsite,
whose three distinctive summits are a prominent landmark in the
Border country.

The lowlands that extend inland from the Solway are
developed on Silurian, Carboniferous and New Red strata. The
last, comprising mainly weak sandstones, along with breccias and
shales, correspond with the low ground at the head of the

Solway, occupy the structural and topographic basins of
Dumfries and Lochmaben, survive in the upper part of the Annan
valley, and accord with the strip of low ground between Luce Bay
and Loch Ryan. Along the course of the middle Nith are two
further basins, each entirely surrounded by uplands except along
the course of the river itself. The more southerly, the Thornhill
basin, contains New Red and Carboniferous rocks, while the
Sanquhar basin has only Carboniferous rocks (fig. 1.6).

Highlands and islands
Although the Scottish Highlands include numerous summits
standing higher than any other part of the British Isles, they are
bordered by considerable lowlands in the east. The islands show
much variety, some being entirely mountainous, others barely
rising above the sea, and yet others combining mountain and
lowland.

Figure 1.7 shows a division of the Highlands and islands into
four main types of landform. This map is in some respects similar

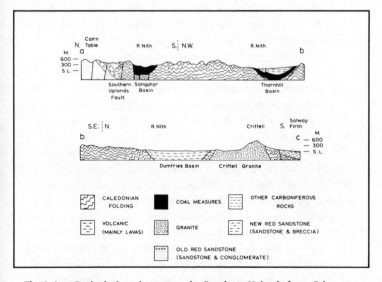

Fig. 1.6   Geological section across the Southern Uplands from Cairn
Table to the Solway.

to a map produced by Linton (1951a) although it was constructed independently. In the west is an area that, despite very varied
geology and relief, has a unity in having been severely affected by
glacial erosion to produce an extremely irregular rocky landscape
and a highly indented coastline. Yet despite this intense glacial
activity, the area retains distinct remains of plateaux on many
interfluves. This area, whose variable upper limit does not exceed
about 600 m, gives way eastwards to mountainous country, the
junction often being abrupt. The mountain belt, with many
summits exceeding 900 m, has been greatly dissected, especially
by glacial action: deep valleys separate mountain ridges, each of
which is divided by cols, often glacially emphasised, into a series
of summits. Although a general accordance of summit level may
be noted from a high vantage point, the mountains often
culminate in sharp crests or peaks and are often deeply bitten
into by corries.

The mountain area is succeeded eastwards, sometimes along an
identifiable line, sometimes after a zone of transition, by a much
more massive type of relief that is especially well developed in a
large area of the Grampians. Plateaux are widespread and ridges
and peaks infrequent. In much of the Grampians altitudes in this
plateau country are comparable with those in the western
mountains, but in the northern Grampians and still more so in the
northern Highlands the general plateau altitude declines northwards. In the extreme north of the mainland the plateau is barely
distinguishable from the Caithness lowland. This lowland and
others along the east coast comprise the fourth landform type
shown in figure 1.7.

The distribution of the four landform types is in some
instances related to geological factors but it often disregards
them. However, especially at a local scale, geology has had much
influence on the relief of the Highlands and islands.

In Caithness and along the Moray Firth coasts the lower ground
is underlain mainly by sandstones of Old Red age. However, Old
Red conglomerates are associated with some prominent features,
such as the pronounced scarp of Ben Horn in eastern Sutherland
(fig. 1.8), the sharp conical hill of Maiden Pap (484 m) and the
larger conical mass of Morven (705 m) in Caithness. Although the

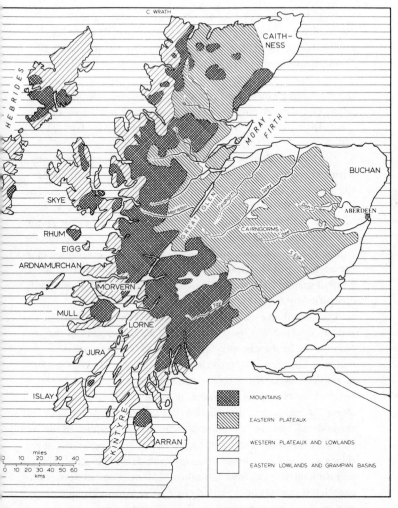

Fig. 1.7   Principal morphological divisions of the Highlands and islands.

surface on which the Old Red strata were deposited has been disrupted by faulting it is clear that it had considerable relief. The most extreme evidence of this is the quartzite ridge of Scaraben (626 m) in Caithness, for Old Red breccias representing cemented screes cling to the slopes of the mountain, implying that it is essentially an ancient feature (Crampton *et al.* 1914). In the northeast Grampians the location of Old Red outliers, some of them extremely small (fig. 1.1), implies that some valleys are in part ancient features of structural or erosional origin. A map of the exhumed elements in the present land surface in the vicinity of the Old Red outcrops has been constructed for the area northwards from the neighbourhood of the Great Glen by Godard (1965).

The Buchan lowland is mainly developed across resistant metamorphic and igneous rocks, its most conspicuous feature being the solitary quartzite mass of Mormond Hill rising to 240 m. The Peterhead granite is entirely associated with low ground, while lowland and low hills around Aberdeen are also formed of granite. Yet some distance west of Aberdeen the latter granite rises as the Hill of Fare to a pronounced plateau at about 470 m, which marks the beginning of the Grampian plateau country. Bennachie is another granite hill overlooking the Buchan lowland, its summit, diversified by tors, reaching 528 m.

The Dalradian metamorphic rocks that constitute much of the Buchan lowland also form some of the highest ground in the Grampians. In the east they are associated with extensive plateaux but they also form the most striking mountains in the Grampians. Quartzite is one of the most resistant rocks. In the heart of the Grampians it is seen in a series of mountains rising above 900 m, such as The Cairnwell, Cairn Mairg, Ben-a-Ghlo and the isolated, steep-sided, pointed ridge of Schiehallion. In the Ben Nevis area it forms a series of distinctive pointed peaks and sharp ridges such as Stob Choire Easain, Am Bodach, Sgurr a'Mhaim and Binnein Mòr at around 1000 to 1100 m. Another very resistant rock is the metamorphosed grit that accords with bold peaks such as Ben Lomond, Ben Ledi, Ben Vorlich and Ben Chonzie along the southern edge of the Highlands. Relatively weak rocks include the Dalradian metamorphosed shales and limestones, which usually form relatively low ground. The limestone outcrops are sometimes pocked with sink holes and in places have been eroded into small rock basins by glacier ice.

Granite outcrops provide further variety in the Grampians. The

Cairngorm granite corresponds with a bulky mass of high ground, steep slopes leading up to an undulating plateau that attains 1200 to 1300 m. South of the Dee, Lochnagar and Mount Keen are the highest parts of two other granite masses and stand boldly above nearby plateaux developed mainly on metamorphic rocks. The granite of Ben Rinnes near the lower Spey exceeds in altitude any adjacent ground, while in the west the outcrop of the Etive granite accords with massive uplands culminating in Ben Starav and Ben Cruachan. On the other hand, the Rannoch granite, although forming some high ground, floors much the greater part of an extensive basin in the heart of the Grampians. The basin occupies some 400 km^2 and its floor, situated mainly between 300 and 400 m, is surrounded by mountains that reach 900 to 1000 m.

Inland from Oban, Old Red lavas cover an extensive area that barely exceeds 500 m at its highest points. Irregular hills, innumerable rocky knobs and small steep-sided glens characterise this area. Stepped hill sides reflect successive lava flows but individual scarps extend only short distances owing to frequent faults. Southeast of the volcanic outcrop, from Loch Awe to the northern part of the Kintyre peninsula, marked contrasts in rock resistance have been exploited by glacier ice to produce parallel ridges and hollows aligned northeast and southwest with the strike of the rocks. Epidiorite is the most resistant rock and forms elongated rocky ridges. The thicker quartzites also form craggy ridges in places, but alternating elongated outcrops of quartzite and epidiorite are often associated with hollows on the former and ridges on the latter. Limestones form low smooth slopes while schists and phyllites occupy the lowest ground. Dykes provide minor variations, some according with small ridges and others with clefts and gullies (Peach *et al.* 1909).

The northwestern Grampians are formed of Moinian metamorphic rocks that tend to be associated with broad massive hills of rather similar appearance to each other except where igneous rocks introduce variety. West of the Spey the Moine rocks constitute an extensive area of rolling peat-covered plateau country that falls gently northwards from about 900 to about 600 m. Much of the Highlands north of the Great Glen is formed of Moine rocks and includes impressive mountain areas as well as rather monotonous tracts of modest relief. The pelitic rocks tend to correspond with the more impressive scenery, with bolder mountains and sharper ridges, and in Easter Ross form the large mass of Ben Wyvis (1045 m) that stands high above surrounding ground.

The northwest coastlands of Scotland in a belt extending for 180 km from Cape Wrath and Loch Eriboll to eastern Skye are characterised by remarkable and contrasting landforms unequalled elsewhere in the British Isles. These forms are intimately related to the geology. The Lewisian gneiss, severely folded, metamorphosed, and intruded by igneous rocks, forms the basement (fig. 1.8). On the highly irregular eroded surface of the gneiss rests a great thickness of (pre-Cambrian) Torridon sandstone, which often has only a slight dip. The Torridonian (and Lewisian) rocks are cut across by a relatively smooth, inclined unconformity at the base of the Cambrian-Ordovician strata, which comprise quartzite overlain by limestone. This rock

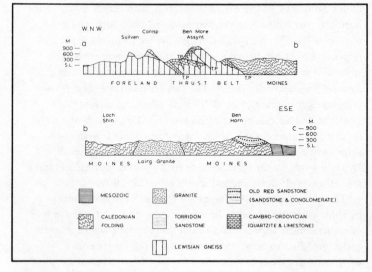

Fig. 1.8   Geological section across the Northern Highlands from near Lochinver to near Brora. T.P. Thrustplane.

sequence applies to a belt 15 to 35 km wide (measured from the outer coast) that is terminated on its eastern side by major thrust planes that mark the edge of the Caledonian orogenic belt. Within the area of thrusting the rocks have been broken into slices that have (in relative terms) over-ridden each other westwards, so that the simple sequence Lewisian/Torridonian/Cambrian-Ordovician no longer applies (fig. 1.8).

The Lewisian gneiss usually crops out on the lower ground, although in places it extends up to altitudes exceeding 800 m. It has been subjected to powerful glacial erosion and forms extremely irregular terrain. Rocky knobs and hills, often ice-smoothed and ice-plucked, alternate with irregular hollows containing peat or lakes. On the ground the landscape looks chaotic, but aerial photographs reveal a strong lineation of features from southeast to northwest corresponding with the principal faults, shatter belts, dykes and igneous sheets. In marked contrast the overlying Torridon sandstone forms conspicuous mountains on whose steep slopes the successive beds of grit and sandstone appear in regular steps. Well-developed vertical jointing has favoured the production of steep-walled corries while the joints and bedding planes have permitted the formation of massive buttresses and stepped cones. The higher Torridonian mountains rise to between 600 and 1000 m and their characteristics are well displayed in the Ben Bhan range, but the most remarkable feature is isolated Suilven which rises precipitously on all sides from a Lewisian gneiss lowland to 731 m.

In the eastern parts of the area the quartzite appears as a highly resistant capping to mountains composed mainly of Torridon sandstone. The quartzite forms sharp ridges and symmetrical pointed peaks, the white rock standing in marked contrast to the red-brown of the underlying sandstone. Quartzite cappings occur, for example, on Canisp (fig. 1.8), Quinag, An Teallach, Beinn Eighe and the three peaks of Liathach, all of which rise to between 800 and 1070 m. In other places the quartzite forms dip slopes that may descend rapidly through a vertical interval of several hundred metres, as on the great asymmetrical ridge west of Loch Eriboll. The overlying limestones are associated with small areas of karstic scenery involving caves, sink holes, swallow holes and underground streams as around Durness and Inchnadamph.

The various islands distributed to the west and north of the mainland display great variations in relief and geology. The north-south grain of the highly-folded metamorphic and igneous rocks of the Shetland Islands accords with a pronounced series of parallel ridges and depressions, limestone especially being associated with the latter. The highest point in the islands, Ronas Hill (450 m), occurs on a granite mass in northern Mainland. The Orkney Islands are mainly a gently undulating lowland developed on Old Red sedimentary rocks. The only significant relief is in Hoy, where resistant Old Red sandstones belonging to a group that does not occur elsewhere in the islands form steep hills with rounded outlines. Much of the long island chain of the Outer Hebrides, extending for over 200 km, is a glacially-eroded low-land developed across Lewisian gneiss. Narrow irregular marine inlets penetrate to the heart of most islands, small lakes abound and peat is widespread. The lowland is diversified by isolated hills that often rise abruptly from it, such as Eaval (347 m) in North Uist and Hecla and Beinn Mhor in South Uist (over 600 m). The southern part of the Isle of Lewis is a severely dissected hill and mountain area (Clisham, 799 m) partly developed on the Lewisian gneiss and partly on granite.

Among the inner islands Jura is almost entirely quartzite and is essentially a glacially-eroded plateau-like mass above which the Paps of Jura (784 m) rise in bold isolation, while the higher parts of adjacent Islay are also formed mainly of quartzite. The land-forms of the other principal islands close to the Scottish mainland, and of some of the minor ones, are related to powerful Tertiary igneous activity. Plateau lavas cover extensive areas in Skye and Mull, and on the mainland adjacent to Mull have a con-siderable outcrop in Morvern. Individual flows are usually less than 15 m thick, but the total thickness of the lavas is great: at least 1800 m in Mull for example. Stepped plateaux and stepped hill sides relate to individual flows, differential erosion being facilitated by the slaggy tops and bottoms of the flows and sometimes by weathering that occurred in the intervals between successive lava outpourings. In northern Skye the basalt lavas form a great east-facing escarpment culminating in The Storr (719 m). Jurassic strata, especially shales, underlie the basalt, as a result of which huge masses of rock have moved down along curved slip planes, a belt up to two kilometres wide at the foot of the scarp consisting of a chaotic mass of tilted blocks, crags and pinnacles, with intervening hollows that sometimes contain small lakes (F.W. Anderson and Dunham 1966).

In northern Skye and in southern Raasay Tertiary sills form scarps amid the weaker Mesozoic strata, while in southern Arran they project similarly from the New Red strata into which they were injected. In the island of Eigg dolerite sills and basalt lavas alternate, giving a stepped landscape in which the sills stand out, the island being crowned by the steep-sided columnar pitchstone mass of the Sgurr of Eigg. Thousands of Tertiary dykes are known in the inner islands and the adjacent mainland, a few of them continuing far beyond this area. Some form straight, narrow ridges or hollows, according to their resistance relative to the rocks that border them. They cross the island of Lismore in Loch Linnhe as low ridges above the surrounding Dalradian limestone, while in many coastal locations in western Scotland they form straight wall-like features running out to sea.

Only the roots now remain of the Tertiary central volcanoes but they usually form high ground, being mainly resistant intrusive igneous rocks. In Skye a mass of gabbro forms the Cuillins with a series of jagged peaks exceeding 900 m. By comparison the adjacent Red Hills, composed of granophyre and granite, appear relatively smooth but nevertheless include pointed peaks. The mountains of eastern Mull correspond with an igneous complex although Ben More, the highest point of the island (966 m), is composed of plateau basalts. In the Ardnamurchan peninsula the most interesting correlation between geology and relief is provided by one of the ring complexes. Here a major ring-dyke is associated with an almost circular belt of hills some 5 km across with steep inward-facing slopes and crags. Within the enclosed lowland another ring-dyke forms a low circular ridge surrounding a small central knob. The mountainous southern part of Rhum, rising abruptly from the sea to culminate in Askival (810 m), is formed of intrusive rocks representing the roots of one of the

Tertiary central volcanoes, while the mountainous granite area of northern Arran marks the site of another. In Arran the coarser-grained granite is associated with rugged pointed mountains while the finer-grained type accords with more rounded and generally lower features. To the south of Arran a Tertiary intrusion forms the tiny solitary island of Ailsa Craig that rises sharply from the Firth of Clyde to an altitude of more than 300 m. Much more isolated, beyond the Outer Hebrides, St Kilda and Boreray are fragments of another central volcano and, far out in the Atlantic, Rockall is the minute visible part of another mass of Tertiary igneous rock.

2 Tertiary landform evolution

Cover rocks

In part the relief of the Highlands and Southern Uplands is of very ancient origin in that it has been exhumed from beneath a cover of pre-Tertiary rocks. The significance in this respect of certain Old Red outcrops in the northeast Grampians and between the Great Glen and Caithness was mentioned in chapter 1. In the Southern Uplands Lauderdale appears to be an ancient valley from which the Old Red strata have not been completely removed, while farther west the deep narrow valley of the upper Annan is the most striking example of an old depression containing New Red strata. The oldest exhumed features are in northwest Scotland, where pre-Cambrian hills and valleys with a relief amplitude of several hundred metres have been partly exhumed from beneath Torridon sandstone (Peach *et al.* 1913a). All these features are of local significance, however.

Exhumation on a broad scale is implied by the relations of cover rocks to the older folded rocks of the Highlands and Southern Uplands. It has long been inferred from glacial erratics that Mesozoic rocks that crop out on the Moray Firth coasts occur widely beneath the firth itself. This is now supported by the existence of a large negative gravity anomaly (Flinn 1969a) and confirmed by boreholes in the sea-bed. Similar rocks have been proved to occur not far off-shore farther south along the east coast of Scotland. A major Mesozoic basin lies between the Outer Hebrides and the mainland and extensive areas of Mesozoic strata occur farther south on the sea floor (Binns *et al.* 1973). Tiny outcrops of these rocks occur along the coast of northwest Scotland while they are widely preserved on land in the west in association with the Tertiary igneous rocks. Another major sedimentary basin lies beneath the Solway Firth and a smaller one corresponds with Luce Bay (Bott 1968). This and associated evidence suggest that a large part of the coast of Scotland is related in its main outlines (and sometimes in considerable detail) to the juxtaposition of relatively weak and relatively resistant strata. It may also be inferred that, at least in the west, much of the removal of Mesozoic strata has taken place since the Tertiary lavas were ejected, for to argue otherwise would be to attribute to a remarkable coincidence the fact that they are preserved extensively on land in the west only where protected by the Tertiary igneous rocks. It may also be suggested that the steep western face of the Northern Highlands, 600 to 900 m high and extending for 200 km southwards from the vicinity of Cape Wrath, is in its main outlines an exhumed Mesozoic feature (Sissons 1967a).

On the other hand, it cannot be assumed that the removal of Mesozoic and older rocks (especially the Old Red strata) from the Highlands and Southern Uplands resulted in the exhumation of the present plateaux. This type of interpretation has been proposed for the Welsh and Pennine plateaux. In Scotland it was favoured by Barrow *et al.* (1912), who suggested that the plateau of the southeast Grampians has been exhumed from beneath Old Red strata, Lochnagar and Mount Keen rising above it having possessed approximately their present form in Old Red times. Such an interpretation ignores the topographic and structural complexity of the base of the Old Red. As George (1955) has pointed out, it is also inapplicable in the Southern Uplands, where the basins containing New Red and/or Carboniferous strata are highly discordant to the plateau surface.

Planation surfaces

A. Geikie (e.g. 1901) stressed the accordance of summits in the Highlands and Southern Uplands and emphasised the great contribution of Tertiary erosion to the formation of the 'tableland'. Later workers who have studied planation surfaces fall into two main groups, one favouring a marine origin and giving a limited vertical range (or no range at all) for specific surfaces, the other supporting a subaerial origin and assigning a greater altitudinal range to individual surfaces.

The marine hypothesis is more than a century old but recent studies were initiated by Hollingworth (1938), who considered southwest Scotland as part of a larger area. Based on map analyses Hollingworth suggested the existence of planation surfaces at 790-820, 325, 220-245, 170 and 120 m, proposing their formation by marine agency when relative stillstands interrupted a period of general emergence. George (1955), in a study of the westcentral Southern Uplands, used projected profiles to portray horizontal planation surfaces at 810, 700, 510, 325 and 180 m. In the Central Lowlands he identified benches at 700, 580, 510, 325 and 180 m (George 1960). Subsequently (1966) he constructed projected profiles for Arran, Mull, Skye and parts of the adjacent mainland. Although allowing the possibility of slight warping, he illustrated horizontal surfaces over this large area at 970, 730 and 490 m, arguing that they are of marine origin. The concept of horizontal marine planation surfaces was also supported by Jardine (1959, 1966), who identified them in the western Southern Uplands at 790-850, 580-610, 520-550, 410-425, 300-335, 230-260, 180-215, 135-150 and 60 m. He suggested that the features at 300-335 and 180-215 m are equivalent to platforms at these altitudes occurring elsewhere in Great Britain. Walton (1963) suggested that planation surfaces in northeast Scotland below 335 m may be of marine origin and identified them at 300, 260-300, 150-230, below 120, and 60-75 m.

Planation surfaces with a broad range of altitude were mentioned by Peach and Horne in various publications. The High Plateau, above which monadnocks rose, was placed between 600 and 900 m, while the Intermediate Plateau was considered to have an upper limit of about 300 m. The most widely quoted work is the cartographic study of Fleet (1938) on a large area of the Grampians. He described the Grampian Main Surface at 730-940 m (above which rose monadnocks such as the Cairngorms and Lochnagar), the Grampian Lower Surface at 460-640 m, and the Grampian Valley Benches (of relatively small extent) at 230-300 m. In the western Ochils Soons (1958) identified planation surfaces at 460-580 and 230-300 m. Sugden (1968) referred to marked breaks of slope at 760 and 910 m in the western Cairngorms as well as to a surface at about 1070-1220 m. The most

detailed work on Scottish planation surfaces is by Godard (1965),
who studied a large area in the northern mainland along with
various islands. His surfaces lie at 700-940, 610-700, 400-610,
180-300 and 90-180 m.

The altitudes given by Fleet and Godard are very similar (a
similarity enhanced when it is noted that Godard's 610-700 m
feature is a minor one), they partly agree with those of Soons and
Sugden, and they are in general accord with the views of Peach
and Horne. On the other hand, although Hollingworth, George
and Jardine each provided data relating to the western Southern
Uplands, only the highest surface (which is merely the highest
points of the area) and the feature just above 300 m was recognised by all three of them. The broad altitude ranges given by the
former group seem more realistic when one considers the visible
variability of Scottish planation surfaces and the complications introduced by variable rock resistance and by glaciation. The horizontality of planation surfaces of small altitudinal range (or of
no stated range) over large areas, as portrayed by the group
favouring marine erosion, seems very improbable, for it is difficult to believe that large areas of complex structure broken by
major faults have been involved in relative uplift of hundreds of
metres without significant distortion. Neither is horizontality in
accord with the evidence of warping of a Quaternary marine
platform that exists in western Scotland (p. 119). Present
instability is indicated by minor earthquakes, especially along the
Great Glen, Highland Boundary and Ochil faults, while the great
thickness of Tertiary and Quaternary sediments (perhaps exceeding 3500 m) in the North Sea basin revealed by the oil and gas
investigations implies major subsidence of that basin during
Tertiary and Quaternary times that could hardly have failed to
result in significant tilting of considerable areas of Scotland.

Such evidence also suggests that the similar planation surface
altitudes given by the investigators cited above who favour a subaerial origin of these surfaces does not necessarily mean that
tilting has not occurred. Godard in fact attributed the gradients
of his surfaces partly to warping (which helps to account for the
impression of merging features given by his overall altitude ranges
quoted above). Flinn (1969b) suggested tilting of northern Scot-

land from quite different evidence. He stated that seawards from the base of the present cliffs there is usually a less steep slope, which is normally concave upwards and in places stepped. This slope ends at the final break of slope beyond which the sea floor is flat or gently rolling. The final break of slope descends northwards from about -55 m off the Buchan coast to about -80 m off Shetland. Flinn suggested that the submarine slope is a result of marine erosion, the whole area being in a relatively submerged state with a slight tilt to the north.

It is often assumed that the planation surface remnants that now survive in Scotland have been relatively little modified since their original formation. Yet the evidence for differential erosion described in chapter 1 implies otherwise, for it indicates that in many parts of Scotland present altitudes are related to the nature of the rocks. Furthermore, the widely-used argument that plateau remnants and spur crest flats at accordant altitude on different types of rock indicate the presence of an planation surface is questionable, for it can be argued, especially for the higher altitudes, where differential erosion has presumably operated longest, that such accordances may well point to the opposite conclusion where the rocks involved vary considerably in their resistance to erosion. Thus, while there is no doubt that planation surfaces exist in many parts of Scotland it is far from established how individual remnants relate to each other.

While supporters of the marine origin of planation surfaces are clear about the formative agent, supporters of the subaerial hypothesis are much less specific. Both groups have given little attention to the possible significance of slope retreat in the manner envisaged by W. Penck and L.C. King, yet it can provide a link between the apparently contradictory hypotheses (Sissons 1960). The formation of an extensive subaerial planation surface implies the contemporaneous development of a marine planation surface in suitable locations. With subsequent uplift the valley slopes and marine cliffs bounding such features may be envisaged as continuing to retreat, while a new surface of subaerial and marine origin is developed at a lower level. With further uplift the process is repeated. On this hypothesis marine planation surfaces are unlikely to occur (owing to destruction by slope retreat)

except at low levels, the earliest planation surfaces having probably been totally extinguished by the encroachment of later features. The high steep slopes of resistant rock bounding weak rock
lowlands represent locations where slope retreat has been so re-
tarded that successive waves retreating relatively rapidly across
the weak rocks have merged into each other.

Deposits that might provide clues as to the origin of planation
surfaces or the climatic conditions prevailing when they were
formed are of very limited extent in Scotland. Leaf beds and
lateric soil horizons preserved between lava flows in western
Scotland indicate a warm temperate climate in early Tertiary
times. They led Linton (1951a) to state that at least the
Grampian Main and Lower surfaces were formed under a warmer
climate than exists today and even to suggest that Mount Keen
may once have been a true inselberg rising above a humid tropical
peneplain (cf. p. 22). Godard (1965) inferred that the climate
was still considerably warmer than today when his lowest surface
was formed, basing his inference on deposits comparable with the
Mediterranean terra rossa (itself related to a warmer climate than
currently prevails in the Mediterranean) found in fissures in the
Cambrian-Ordovician limestone of northwest Scotland. From
other scattered deposits he inferred that uplift and dissection of
this surface coincided with a change to a cool wet climate.

Tiny occurrences of rotten granite have been described from
high ground in the Cairngorms, while on high ground farther
south in the Grampians it has been claimed that decomposed
undisturbed rock up to 12 m thick exists. At much lower eleva-
tions in the northern half of the Scottish mainland rotten rock
has been reported at various localities. Deep weathering has been
described from many points in northeast Scotland, sections in
Aberdeen, for example, showing granite weathered to a depth of
9 m below till that is little weathered (Barrow *et al.* 1913;
Phemister and S. Simpson 1949; Fitzpatrick 1963). In northeast
Scotland two small areas of coarse rounded gravel with chalk
flints, along with beds of sand and sandy clay, lie between 105
and 120 m. A Pliocene age has been tentatively suggested for
them and they are said to rest on a rock platform that may be of
marine origin (Read 1923). These numerous small scattered

deposits of various types have given rise to a considerable amount
of speculation but their significance still remains uncertain.

On the other hand, the evidence of powerful Tertiary erosion
provided by the Tertiary igneous rocks has long been appreciated
(e.g. A Geikie 1901). Radiometric dating shows that the major
extrusive and intrusive activity occurred 55 to 70 million years
ago in early Tertiary times. The lava areas that now remain are
the remnants of vast plateaux that have been disrupted by
faulting and warping and also by erosion. In Arran the former
existence of plateau lavas can be inferred from remanié masses.
and fragments in a subsidence caldera. The central volcanoes that
once existed have been worn down to their roots along with
associated calderas kilometres in diameter. In Rhum and Skye it
appears that around 1000 m of cover rocks have been removed
from the plutonic masses. The significance of this great erosion
has been stressed by George (1966), whose reconstructed section
across Arran suggests that some 2500 m of rock have been
removed in Tertiary times from above the present summits of the
granite mountains. Such erosion, often of resistant igneous rocks
that, despite it, still form high ground, can hardly have been
restricted to the Tertiary igneous province. One must therefore
infer that high-level planation surfaces of early Tertiary origin
cannot be present in the land surface today.

Further evidence is provided by the Tertiary dykes, a few of
which extend, with a general northwest and southeast trend,
across the whole country. Radiometric dating indicates that they
are 50-55 million years old. They occur as high as 900 m in the
Highlands and up to an altitude of 600 m in the Southern
Uplands. This implies that valleys had not been excavated below
these altitudes in the respective areas when dyke injection
occurred. Furthermore, since there are no associated lava flows
(away from the main volcanic areas), it would be remarkably
fortuitous if the present highest points attained by the dykes
were just below any lava flows that once existed. Hence it is
likely that, at the time of dyke intrusion, valley floors were considerably above the altitudes now attained by the dykes. Thus the
present valleys of Scotland in areas where Tertiary dykes occur
(and inferentially elsewhere) have been entirely formed since

dyke intrusion ceased. Valley formation in later Tertiary times is implied by the fact that most valleys in the Scottish uplands, despite glaciation, are relatively narrow.

Drainage initiation

The origin of the drainage system of Scotland has for long given rise to speculation and considerable differences of opinion still exist. A. Geikie (1865), in discussing the Tay drainage, seems to have been the first to suggest an early river system flowing southeast, but it was Mackinder (1902) who developed this idea. Mackinder suggested that the drainage was initiated on a subaerially-fashioned land surface tilted to the southeast. Some of the initial southeastward-flowing rivers thereafter turned eastwards to become the Tyne of northern England and the Tweed. The concept of initial southeastward streams was supported by Peach and Horne (1910, 1930). They considered gaps in the Pentland Hills to have been cut by such streams, explaining the anomalous eastward-flowing Tweed as a subsequent stream despite the discordant relationship to geology displayed by part of its course. Mort (1918) mapped a system of rivers flowing southeastwards across Kintyre, southern Scotland and the Solway, the sources and destinations of these postulated rivers being obscure. Linton (1933) pointed out that the Mackinder hypothesis failed to explain the discordant streams flowing northwards to the Tweed and its tributary the Teviot, while Bremner (1942) justifiably argued that a new drainage system would not be developed by uplift and tilting of a subaerially-formed surface.

A second group of interpretations involves initial eastward-flowing streams, an idea first hinted at by Ramsay (1878). Not long afterwards Cadell (1886) reconstructed a system of such headstreams for the Forth. Bailey *et al.* (1916) mapped an original eastward-flowing drainage system on either side of Loch Linnhe. Bremner (1942) considered a large area of Scotland and postulated initial eastward-directed streams some of whose sources lay west of the present mainland coastline. He believed that the drainage was developed on a mantle of Cretaceous rocks, the initial simple pattern being modified during emergence by faulting and warping in the Moray Firth and west of the mainland.

The best known contribution in this group is that of Linton
(1951a), who developed Bremner's interpretation. He maintained
that the present drainage was initiated at the beginning of the
Tertiary era as a layer of newly-deposited chalk was uplifted
from beneath the sea. Over most of Scotland south of the Great
Glen the chalk was tilted to the east, some of the streams that
developed on its surface now being represented by the whole or

Fig. 2.1   The earliest British rivers, according to Linton (1951a). Continuous lines represent rivers presumed to be consequent on the initial
post-Cretaceous uplift and eastward tilt. Broken lines represent the possible
independent or later drainage of the Moray Firth depression.

parts of the Isla-Deveron-Ugie, Avon-Don, Feshie-Geldie-Dee, Tummel-South Esk, Lyon-Tay, Lochay-Almond, Balva-Earn, Devon-Leven, Forth and Tweed. Some of these eastward-flowing consequent streams, most notably the Tweed, received consequent tributaries, while a system of southeastward-flowing consequents joined a postulated east-flowing Solway river whose beheaded remnant is now the Tyne. In northern Scotland an initial system of rivers converging on the Moray Firth was envisaged (fig. 2.1). The unconformity at the base of the chalk (the sub-Cenomanian surface) was considered to have had negligible relief and Linton believed that it is represented by the most easterly high points of the present land surface, which have probably suffered no erosion since the chalk was removed. Thus the sub-Cenomanian surface was depicted as rising from 450 m in the vicinity of Aberdeen to about 1200 m in the Cairngorms, where the summit plateau was considered to be a possible remnant of it (fig. 2.2). On the other hand, in the west of Scotland the chalk now lies far below the Highland summits and is often below sea-level, being preserved beneath the Tertiary lavas. Linton therefore argued that the drainage of Scotland was initiated on the eastern flank of a great arch with a northsouth axis, the central part of the arch having subsequently collapsed in association with the Tertiary igneous activity to produce a major rift whose floor may be as much as 1500 m below the original level.

Unfortunately this attractively simple hypothesis meets certain difficulties. Thus the idea of the sub-Cenomanian surface surviving on the Cairngorms and elsewhere is inconsistent with the evidence of vast Tertiary erosion demonstrated in the Tertiary igneous province. The reconstructed sub-Cenomanian surface portrayed at altitudes up to 900 m over the Moray Firth (fig. 2.2) ignored the evidence from glacial erratics implying that chalk occurs below sea-level here, an implication now confirmed by borehole investigations. George (1966) denied the existence of the rift envisaged by Linton and also argued that, since the chalk in western Scotland has a maximal residual thickness of less than 5 m, it is slight evidence on which to infer a contemporaneous drowning of all the Highland region.

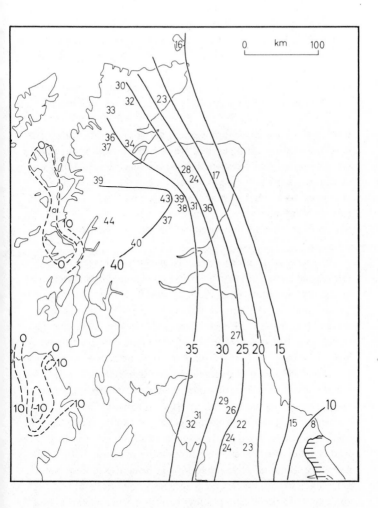

Fig. 2.2   Elements in the reconstruction of the earliest British land surface, according to Linton (1951a). Heights (in hundreds of feet) of the surviving most easterly high summits are shown, along with contours of a smooth surface that would touch these summits. Approximate contours (in hundreds of feet) of the base of the Antrim and Hebridean lavas are suggested. In eastern England part of the outcrop of the Cenomanian strata is marked.

A variation of the eastward-flowing stream hypothesis was proposed by Holgate (1969) for the ground on either side of the Great Glen. He elaborated Kennedy's (1946) idea of major trans-current movement on the Great Glen fault, arguing that a sinistral shift of 134 km in Old Red times was followed by a dextral shift of 29 km after the Tertiary dykes were injected. Holgate believed the drainage was initiated in early Tertiary times on a more or less even eastward-sloping surface of unspecified origin and was later dislocated by the dextral movement along the fault. Additional drainage modifications resulted from river captures induced by a series of broad shallow folds. It was also suggested (echoing one of Linton's (1951a) diagrams) that a mean downthrow to the northwest of about 180 m was associated with the dextral shift. Holgate's arguments are unconvincing, however, and the geo-morphic evidence he presented can be interpreted quite differently.

A third type of interpretation relating to drainage origins, introduced by Hollingworth (1938) was applied by George in a series of publications (e.g. 1955, 1965, 1966). The latter argued that by mid-Tertiary times Scotland had been considerably dis-sected by erosion, the Central Lowlands already being significant-ly developed; that submergence of the whole country followed; and that during later pulsed uplift marine surfaces were produced on which the present drainage system was initiated. This hypo-thesis allows the varied directions of discordant streams to be explained as also the fact that most such streams flow away from high ground. However, it introduces a vast submergence for which there is no direct geological evidence. It also means that, since the land is believed to have been considerably dissected before sub-mergence, the river system developed during the subsequent emergence would not be an entirely new one but would be largely guided by the pre-existing valleys (unless marine planation be postulated on a scale now no longer considered acceptable).

While difficulties encountered by the three main hypotheses on drainage initiation have been indicated, this is not meant to imply that these hypotheses should be completely rejected. Rather is it suggested that aspects of each can be combined in a fourth hypothesis (Sissons 1967a). George (1966) emphasised that the Tertiary lavas were poured out over a lowland. He referred to possible gentle undulations of hill and valley and to 'the low-lying matured flats of broad basins' related to evidence of swamps and shallow lakes. This lowland must have been extensive for nowhere in the large area of occurrence of the lavas has evidence been found to indicate that they flowed into the sea. The lowland was developed mainly across deformed Mesozoic strata but it was partly on resistant older rocks including Moinian. It therefore seems probable that at this time the adjacent parts of the Highlands (at least) had subdued relief. Already at this early date a drainage system must have been in existence and, since the relation of the Tertiary lavas to the underlying rocks shows that in the igneous province Mesozoic strata had already been removed in places, it may be inferred that such strata had suffered similarly in the then exposed parts of the Highlands. Hence the surface on which the earliest streams began to flow is even older and may well have been composed of chalk and earlier Mesozoic rocks uplifted from beneath the sea towards the end of Cretaceous times, an interpretation approximating to that of Linton. There is no proof that Mesozoic strata covered Scotland but it may be noted that the present low altitude of these rocks in the west is in large measure a result of Tertiary earth movements and Tertiary erosion: before these occurred the surface of the Mesozoic strata in the west stood, in general, much higher in relation to the Highlands than it does now and the former extension of these rocks across the Highlands is more easily envisaged.

The volcanic activity that occurred in Eocene times was associated with warping and major faulting. Although a rift valley was not developed the result was major uplift in the west relative to the igneous province. These events may now be linked with continental drift for Avery *et al.* (1968), on the basis of an aeromagnetic survey of the Norwegian Sea, have shown that Greenland was separating from Norway 60-70 million years ago. The Caledonian fold belt has been traced to the edge of the continental shelf some 50 to 100 km northwest and north of the Shetlands beyond which it is resumed in east Greenland (Watts 1971). Thus early Tertiary separation of Greenland from the Scottish area may have occurred in the vicinity of the shelf

margin, which extends southwestwards to pass 100 km seawards
of the Outer Hebrides.

If allowance is made for drainage modifications, especially
those related to glacial erosion, the present major watershed of
Scotland appears as a simple linear feature (fig. 2.3). In the
northern Highlands it follows the present highest ground and in
the Grampians passes through the Ben Nevis area. In the Central
Lowlands the watershed lies in the plateau country separating
Clyde and Forth drainage, developed (significantly) largely on
Coal Measures that elsewhere in the Central Lowlands form low
ground. In the heart of the Southern Uplands it is situated in the
Tweedsmuir Hills where Broad Law, like Merrick well to the west
and The Cheviot well to the east, rises above 800 m. These
summit accordances are misleading, however, for Merrick is
formed of metamorphic rocks and The Cheviot of granite whereas
Broad Law is composed of weaker sedimentary rocks. Thus, it
may be inferred that before differential erosion occurred the
Tweedsmuir Hills stood much higher relative to Merrick and The
Cheviot. Farther south the watershed is continued by the main
Pennine watershed. Since this simple watershed usually corresponds with the present highest ground it introduces unnecessary
complications to regard it as other than the main initial watershed
of Scotland. Its simple form suggests it approximates the main
axis of uplift of the country. It does not follow, however, that a
simple drainage pattern eastwards and westwards from it was
initiated at one time.

It seems that the earliest rivers of parts of the Highlands were
initiated, as suggested above, towards the end of Cretaceous times
on a cover of Mesozoic rocks, the area subsequently being
reduced to subdued relief by the time Teriary volcanic activity
began. Such early rivers may now be represented by east-flowing
discordant streams in the central Grampians. But there is no hint
in the present land surface here of the eastward slope on which
these streams developed nor is there any justification, in view of
the intensity of Tertiary erosion, for assuming that the early
Teriary lowland is represented by part of the present surface.
Major uplift accompanying the volcanic outpourings accentuated
the main watershed and may have been associated with warping

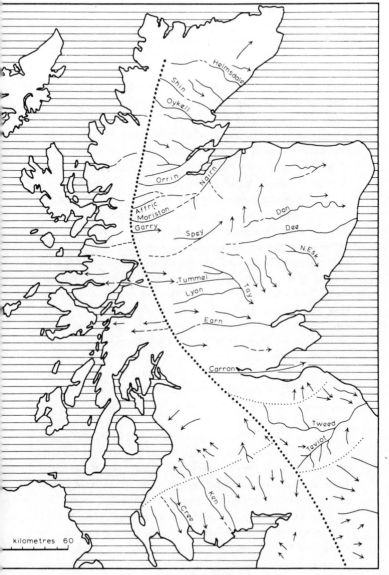

Fig. 2.3   Initial watersheds and initial drainage, according to Sissons (1967a).

in other directions to produce the minor watersheds of southern
Scotland shown in figure 2.3. Tilting towards the North Sea
basin is implied by the sedimentary accumulations of that basin,
while downwarping towards the Moray Firth may also have
occurred. A further factor, however, was marine erosion during
uplift. The way in which cover rocks, extending back to the Old
Red, surround and lap on to the Southern Uplands and the Highlands was described at the beginning of this chapter, as was the
broadly exhumed character of these uplands. Frequently cover
rocks are restricted to a narrow coastal strip or are known to
occur a short distance offshore, implying that the outline of the
present coastline is often a result of removal by the sea of weak
cover rocks from the underlying resistant rocks. It may therefore
be inferred that in the past marine erosion operated in a similar
selective manner at successively lower levels during the emergence
of Scotland. Where the cover rocks were relatively weak, as was
common, marine erosion may have removed them quite rapidly,
thereafter eating far more slowly into the underlying resistant
rocks. With each period of uplift streams would be extended
seawards over the emerging marine benches. Thus the various
directions of the discordant streams of the Scottish uplands may
perhaps be explained along with their tendency to conform with
the regional dip of the cover rocks (or with the inferred dip of
former cover rocks). Marine erosion would have been restricted
to the peripheral parts of the uplands, however, and even here
marine surfaces probably now survive only at low altitudes
owing to slope retreat. Furthermore, with Greenland continuing
to drift away intermittently through Tertiary times on one side
of Scotland (Avery *et al.* 1968) and the North Sea basin sinking
on the other, it is very unlikely that planation surfaces are
horizontal over considerable areas despite an apparent concensus
of opinion to the contrary. The final major event before
glaciation was relatively rapid uplift resulting in the usually
narrow valleys of the uplands, but in the Central Lowlands
slopes had already retreated across the weaker rocks to open up
considerable areas of low ground bordered by steep slopes of
more resistant rock.

3   Glacial landforms

Glacial troughs

Although the principal relief features of Scotland were fashioned
in preglacial times, glaciation resulted in extensive modification
of these features. Glacial landforms occur throughout the country
and only in limited areas are forms obviously related to glacial
action lacking. Erosional landforms predominate, not only in
upland areas but in most lowlands also.

Glacial erosion was most effective in and immediately around
the main areas of ice accumulation. Most important of these by
far was the western Highlands, extending from the vicinity of
Loch Lomond to Loch Broom and largely coincident with the
major area of mountainous terrain shown in figure 1.7. Lesser
centres included the narrow mountain belt in the northernmost
part of the mainland; the mountains of the islands of Lewis,
Skye, Mull and Arran; the Cairngorms; the high ground in the
Grampians lying south of the upper Dee; the Loch Doon area in
the western Southern Uplands; and the Tweedsmuir Hills. There
are variations in the character of the glacial landforms as between
some of these areas however.

In the Cairngorms deep glacial troughs such as glens
Geusachan, Einich and Avon have been cut into the massive
upland and at their heads rise sharply for 300 to 400 m. The steep
rock slopes (sometimes displaying bare granite sheets) that have
resulted from glacial erosion contrast with the undulating plateau
above, yet there is evidence for only one significant rock basin,
which is occupied by Loch Avon. Sugden (1968) suggested that
the granite pseudobedding, which conforms approximately with
the undulations of the plateau surface, developed in relation to
the preglacial relief. Hence where the pseudobedding is present

he inferred that little modification of the preglacial forms has
occurred. Yet it seems possible that the pseudobedding may be
differently explained as related to severe frost action under
periglacial conditions.

South of the Dee the contrast between plateau and glacial
troughs is equally marked. The floors of Glen Clova and its
tributary Glen Doll lie as much as 600-700 m below the nearby
summits in the area where they join. Upstream each glen ends
abruptly at a major rock step above which each is continued by a
much shallower open valley, that above Glen Doll in particular
suggesting a preglacial feature that has suffered little glacial
modification. A pronounced bench on the side of Glen Clova
below its confluence with Glen Doll appears to represent the
little-modified preglacial valley floor into which the glacial trough
was incised. From such evidence Linton (1963) inferred that ice
has cut down as much as 300 m. To the east of Glen Clova
undulating plateau country that is almost everywhere covered
with peat includes valleys 50 to 200 m deep that usually have
only gentle or moderate slopes. In this area, which exceeds
50 km^2, the preglacial relief seems to have been little affected by
glacial action and glacial and fluvioglacial landforms are almost
entirely absent. Yet eastwards the principal valleys of this plateau
country change rapidly in character over a distance of one to two
kilometres to become the glacial troughs of glens Mark and Lee
whose steep walls 300 to 400 m high include precipitous rock
faces. Northwards the undulating plateau is broken by the long
curving gouge of Glen Muick, the south side of which at one
point is a vertical rock face 270 m high. This glen has the only
large proven rock basin (containing Loch Muick) in the southeast
Grampians although another may well be hidden beneath the
drift infill of Glen Clova below the point where Glen Doll joins
it. All these troughs were classified by Linton as Icelandic type,
characterised by ice accumulation on plateau surfaces only
exceptionally dominated by high ground with discharge by steep
ice falls into the ends of valleys dissecting the plateau.

In the western Southern Uplands the Loch Doon area, including the Merrick and Kells ranges, was the main centre of ice
accumulation. The rough rocky glaciated slopes on the meta-

morphic rocks contrast with the typical smooth Southern
Uplands forms while the various rock basins (occupied by lochs
such as Doon, Enoch and Trool) indicate significant glacial
erosion. Major glacial troughs such as occur in the western Highlands are lacking, however, for the belt of high ground bordering
the granite area is narrow, and only short troughs of modest
dimensions exist, such as Glen Trool. In the central Southern
Uplands the characteristic rounded forms of the Tweedsmuir
Hills are abruptly cut off by rougher slopes produced by glacial
erosion. The deep, straight, U-shaped trench occupied by the
Moffat Water follows a major shatter belt and glaciated tributary
valleys hang as much as 200 m above its floor. The Talla reservoir
covers a former lake site occupying a rock basin in the floor of a
short deep glacial trough leading to the Tweed, while the Meggett
Water flows in a more open trough in the opposite direction to
St Mary's Loch, which occupies the only important rock basin in
this area. Other valleys in the Tweedsmuir Hills have clearly been
deepened by ice, but they lack marked rock bars and steps.

In the western Highlands, however, along with the mountain
areas of some of the islands, all the characteristic forms associated
with intense and selective glacial erosion are present in abundance.
The whole area is deeply dissected by interconnected glacial
troughs whose floors are often no more than 100 to 200 m above
sea-level and which, even far into the mountain area, may descend
below sea-level in major rock basins. The mountains are thus
greatly fragmented and, being also bitten into by numerous
corries, often culminate in ridges and peaks. There is considerable
variety between different valleys and also between parts of the
same valley. Glen Lyon, for example, is a long narrow trough that
becomes extremely constricted in the east where it is partly cut in
quartzite, its floor lying 800 to 1000 m below the summits on
either side. In contrast the Tay valley immediately to the south
is far wider, partly because it carried a larger volume of ice and,
along the side of Loch Tay where a broad rock bench suggests as
much as 300 m of vertical ice erosion occurred in the rock basin,
partly because of the presence of relatively weak metamorphosed
limestone. Glen Nevis, whose northern side rises from near sea-
level to the summit of Ben Nevis at 1343 m, varies between a

U-shape and a V-shape with steep and, in places, precipitous walls
for a dozen kilometres or so inland from Fort William, but there-

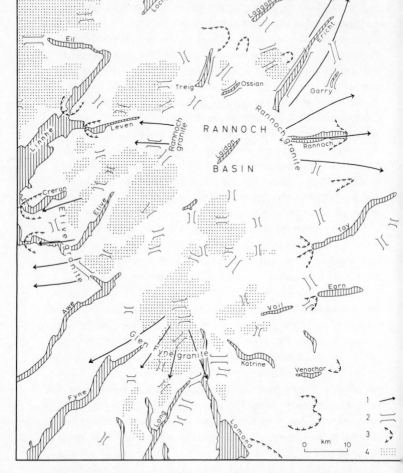

Fig. 3.1   The major centre of ice accumulation in Scotland. Features
shown include principal glacial breaches, direction of transport of certain
erratics, termini of the principal glaciers formed during the Loch Lomond
Readvance, and the area that currently receives more than 2500 mm
precipitation.

after changes to a broad open U with only moderate slopes. Some
valleys are strikingly U-shaped as in the Arran granite, where in
glens Iorsa and Rosa 150 to 250 m of glacial deepening has been
inferred from hanging valleys. Another example is Strath Conon
in the Northern Highlands which, like many other glacial troughs
in the Highlands, follows a major fault.

Along much of the west coast of the Highlands the seaward
parts of many glacial troughs have been drowned by the sea to
form fiords. Gregory (1913) argued at length that the fiords are
tectonic features produced by faulting, an interpretation that was
quickly corrected. In the northwest of the mainland the fiords,
along with other glacially-fashioned smaller coastal indentations,
trend southwest and northeast parallel with the principal geological structures but also with the regional direction of ice movement under ice-sheet conditions. In western Inverness-shire and
northern Argyllshire the fiords vary in direction but have a
general westerly trend in accord with the main ice flow. Farther
south the fiords and lesser inlets trend towards southwest and
south-south-west, partly related to strong geological influence and
partly to ice movement. A general radial pattern is thus displayed
suggesting the diverging flow pattern of an ice-sheet. Linton
(1957) used the fiords and other glacial troughs to identify major
areas of radial flow within the ice-sheet itself, pointing to the
former existence of ice domes such as occur today in the Greenland and Antarctic ice-sheets. The major centre was in the southwest Grampians. In addition to coastal features already
mentioned, Loch Lomond is aligned towards south-south-east,
Loch Katrine towards east-south-east, lochs Voil, Earn, Tay and
Rannoch (along with glens Dochart and Lyon) trend east to
northeast, while lochs Garry, Ericht and Treig trend towards
northeast and north-north-east (fig. 3.1). Linton also described a
similar, though less impressive, pattern of radiating troughs in
Ross-shire.

Glacial breaches

The radial troughs imply modification of the pre-existing relief by
glacial breaching. Breaches abound in the area of intense glacial
erosion in the western Highlands and they also occur (but less

abundantly) in many other parts of Scotland. Linton and Moisley (1960) suggested that the trough occupied by Loch Lomond was essentially produced by glacier ice and replaces an original mainly eastward-directed drainage pattern, a thickness of rock as great as 600 m having been removed by the ice. On the opposite side of the great Grampians ice accumulation area the straight, fault-controlled, 25-km long trench occupied by Loch Ericht breaches the main west-east watershed and was a major routeway for ice flowing from the Rannoch basin to Strathspey (fig. 3.1). Nearly 400 m of downcutting has probably occurred here, while in the similar fault-controlled breach occupied by Loch Treig ice erosion may have amounted to 550 m (Linton 1951b). The trends of some of the major valleys mentioned above do not reflect the regional ice-flow when a large ice-sheet existed, however. Thus, while the Earn, Dochart-Tay and Lyon valleys point to between east and northeast, striae on the intervening uplands as well as numerous glacial breaches indicate a general radial flow towards directions between east and southeast. Hence, at the same time as powerful ice-streams were flowing along the major preglacial valleys, the upper parts of the ice-sheet were moving in a divergent direction across the high ground utilising and deepening minor valleys with suitable trend where they already existed but cutting new ones where such valleys were not available. Among the new features are the breaches at the heads of glens Almond and Lednock, Glen Ogle linking the Dochart and Earn valleys, and the breach between the Lyon and Tay valleys occupied by Lochan na Lairige (where 300 m of ice excavation has probably occurred).

In the mountainous west of the northern Highlands the principal valleys are linked by hundreds of cross cuts produced by glacier ice at high and low levels. In addition, the principal valleys, draining westwards and eastwards from the major north-south watershed, are themselves connected by some thirty major breaches through this watershed. The floors of almost all these major breaches are below 300 m, even though the mountains rise to between 800 and 1200 m. In the south, parts of the mainland have been almost cut off to form islands. Thus Morvern has been almost severed along the line of Loch Sunart, which is continued due east to Loch Linnhe by Glen Tarbert, a mere 11 km long with the highest point on its floor reaching only 100 m above sea-level. Farther north Loch Linnhe bends suddenly to the west as Loch Eil, which is continued westwards by a 6 km strip of low ground that rises to only 18 m, this in turn leading to Loch Shiel, which drains to the west and has a surface altitude of less than 4 m.

Severance has been achieved in the case of Mull, for the Sound of Mull is merely a flooded glacial trough. The same is true of Skye, separated from the mainland by drowned glaciated valleys that narrow to no more than a kilometre. It is very probable that Islay, Jura, Scarba, Luing, Seil and adjacent lesser islands owe their separation from each other to glacial erosion and were all a peninsula of the mainland in preglacial times. The Isle of Bute provides another example, while the adjacent Cumbraes, Lismore and Kerrera in the Firth of Lorne, and Raasay and Scalpay by Skye have probably been similarly detached by selective ice action. In numerous other places further fragmentation into islands has almost occurred. Thus the Kintyre peninsula just fails to be three separate islands and Jura is almost cut in two at Loch Tarbert, while several glacially-eroded low-level hollows cross Mull, Skye and Bute. In the Outer Hebrides the main mountain mass is completely breached at various places, while the existence of the Outer Hebrides as a chain of islands rather than as a single great island is probably almost entirely a result of ice action. A small rise of sea-level would cause additional drowning of glacially-eroded hollows and produce much more fragmentation of the Outer Hebrides.

In the eastern Grampians many small glacial breaches occur as well as some major ones but breaches are less numerous than in the west of Scotland. One of the most impressive is Glen Tilt, a deep straight gash aligned along a major fault where almost 400 m of glacial incision has probably occurred. In the same area the upper Feshie flows eastwards as if to be continued by the Geldie, an eastward-flowing tributary of the Dee with which it is exactly in line. Yet when about to join the Geldie, at which point the two streams differ in altitude by only a metre or two, the Feshie turns abruptly away and descends to the floor of a large glacial breach cut through the former watershed, thereafter continuing to the Spey (fig. 3.2). These anomalous relationships were originally attributed to river capture by adjustment to structure, but Linton (1949) pointed out that the production of the glacial breach resulted in a much lower route being available for the stream that preglacially was the upper Geldie. An even more striking example is provided by the Avon, which flows east-north-east for 20 km before turning abruptly northwards through a glacial breach some 250 m deep. From the sharp bend the Avon valley is continued with the same east-north-east direction by the Don valley in which this stream is initially a pronounced misfit. This was for long accepted as an excellent example of simple river capture but diversion through glacial breaching provides a more satisfactory explanation (Linton 1954).

Several other significant glacial breaches occur in the Cairngorms. One links Glen Derry with Glen Avon through the centre of the mountain mass while others carried ice east and northeast round the southern flanks of the mountains. The best

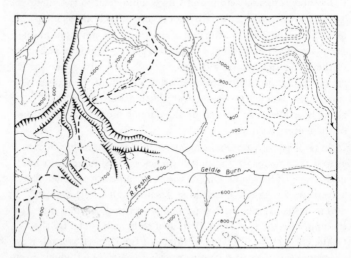

Fig. 3.2   The upper Feshie and Geldie valleys (after Linton 1949). Walls of glacial troughs, the former watershed and supposed remnants of a former valley floor are shown. Contour interval 100 m.

known is the Lairig Ghru which leads straight through the mountains from upper Glen Dee. Linton argued that the Lairig Ghru
was cut by Cairngorms ice nourished in the upper Dee valley.
Sugden (1968), however, found it difficult to understand how
local ice could have breached such high ground (probably over
1100 m initially at the site of the breach) and argued instead that
the breach was cut by an ice-sheet that covered the whole area
and was nourished outside the Cairngorms. The latter interpretation does not accord with the total lack of metamorphic erratics
in this area, which would be readily identifiable on the widespread granite.

The principal glacial breaches in the Central Lowlands are in
the line of volcanic uplands that lies parallel with the Highland
edge. One of these, in the western Ochils, is Glen Eagles, which
leads into the Devon valley. Another ice route crosses obliquely
the hill mass southwest of Stirling, being drained in one direction
by the Endrick and in the other by the Carron. The most
impressive breach is Strathblane, its floor lying less than 100 m
above sea-level except where a volcanic neck forms small steep-
sided Dungoyach in the centre of the valley. Its gently-curving
course reflects the gradually-changing direction of ice movement
and its position and depth the importance of the ice-stream
issuing from the Highlands along the site of Loch Lomond.

Glacial breaches in the Southern Uplands include the Dalveen
Pass in the Lowther Hills and the gap between the Talla reservoir
and the Meggett valley in the heart of the Tweedsmuir Hills. The
Biggar gap, a deep flattish-floored hollow 11 km long linking the
Clyde valley with that of the Tweed, is so little above the present
Clyde that, in exceptional floods, water from the latter finds its
way to the Tweed. The gap was used by Mackinder and Linton to
make the upper Clyde a preglacial tributary of the Tweed now
diverted to the lower Clyde by river capture. Alternatively the
Biggar gap, like the smaller but otherwise similar gap immediately
to the south and parallel to it, is a glacial breach cut by eastward-
moving Southern Uplands ice unable to spread freely into the
Central Lowlands owing to the presence of Highland ice. Another
anomalous feature is the course of the river Nith, for it traverses
the whole breadth of the Southern Uplands, crossing the other-

wise high ground between the Sanquhar and Thornhill basins in a
deep gap that may be a glacial breach.

Rock basins

The constricted, relatively rapid flow of ice through glacial
breaches often resulted in the formation of rock basins, such as
those occupied by lochs Treig and Ericht mentioned above.
Others in the same area are lochs Garry, Ossian and an Duin.
Good examples in Ross-shire are lochs Calavie, Mhoicean and an
Daimh. Small rock basins containing lakes occur in breaches up to
altitudes exceeding 700 m, as in the Ben Nevis area. The effects
of constriction are also seen in the fact that almost all the large
rock basin lakes occupy major valleys in the uplands. The main
concentration is in the western Highlands, where, inland from
Mallaig, by far the deepest lake in the British Isles, Loch Morar,
occurs, with a maximal depth of 310 m, the lowest point on its
floor lying 301 m below sea-level. The concentration in the west
is illustrated in figure 3.3, which is based on data from the survey
carried out by Murray and Pullar (1910), although it should be
noted that this map does not show the important sea-floor basins
or basins now hidden by drift. By far the largest lake basin,
located marginally to the main concentration, is that of Loch
Ness, with a volume of 7,500 million m^3. Its position reflects the
importance of faults in facilitating the excavation of rock basins
for, along with the basins of lochs Oich and Lochy, it forms part
of the trench that follows the Great Glen fault and almost makes
the northern mainland an island. The floor of much of the trench
is well below sea-level, the bottom of Loch Ness, for example,
lying more than 160 m below sea-level for 24 km.

Fault control is also demonstrated in Loch Maree, the largest
lake in the northwest coastlands, for its northeastern side main-
tains an almost straight course for nearly 20 km. This trend is
continued southeastwards for a further 9 km, first by the infilled
head of the loch and then by the deep glacial breach of Glen
Docharty. Lochs Beoraid, Shiel and Laidon occupy fault-guided
rock basins, the last being cut in the floor of the Rannoch basin.
In some instances only a part of a rock basin is fault controlled.
Thus Loch Tay changes direction twice, its middle and deepest

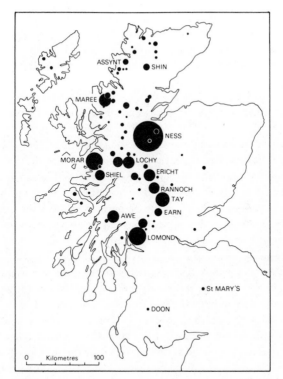

Fig. 3.3   The size of Scottish freshwater lochs as an indicator of the
varying intensity of glacial erosion. Circles are proportional to loch
volumes. Only lochs exceeding 20 million m³ are shown.

section corresponding with a major fault.

The Loch Tay basin begins where two troughs join, suggesting
that overdeepening here relates to the effectiveness of the confluent ice-streams, although a large limestone outcrop may have
facilitated ice erosion. Loch Earn and Loch Morar also commence
where ice-streams became confluent, as do the sea lochs Nevis,
Duich and Broom. Conversely, Loch Avon in the Cairngorms
comes to an end where part of the Glen Avon ice-stream split off
to pass through a glacial breach into Strath Nethy. Some rock
basins were produced in valleys where ice-streams were suddenly
constricted. Thus Loch Brora in eastern Sutherland is situated

where the Brora valley narrows in passing through the Old Red conglomerate and sandstone uplands. Most of the larger Scottish rock basin lakes are typical ribbon lakes, being very long in relation to their width, the latter tending to be fairly constant. Exceptions reflect special local circumstances, with Loch Lomond the most marked. For most of its length this loch occupies a cleft between the mountains that descends to as much as 180 m below sea-level. Towards its southern end, however, it becomes a broad expanse of water rarely more than 30 m deep interrupted by a series of islands. The southward expansion in part reflects the extension of the loch into the Central Lowlands. It also corresponds with the diminution in altitude of the bounding uplands which in turn is partly related to an outcrop of relatively weak Old Red sandstone, the islands being largely composed of resistant conglomerate and metamorphosed grit.

The glacial origin of rock basins was originally proposed more than a century ago by Ramsay, although the great importance of glacial erosion was appreciated long before by Esmark (1827). Ramsay's ideas were elaborated especially by J. Geikie (e.g. 1894), who stressed the importance of the ice-eroded basins beneath the sea off the west coast. On the other hand, Ting (1937) plotted a preglacial river system over the sea bed of this area, while Godard (1965) also mapped river courses over a large area of the continental shelf off western Scotland, as well as in the Moray Firth, interpreting them as preglacial or interglacial features modified by glacial erosion. The early ideas are now supported by new evidence from the sea bed including bathymetric maps and rockhead contour maps.

Some of the sea-floor basins are far more extensive than any that exist on land. Major basins lie between northern Skye and the mainland, between Mull and Jura, and between Arran and the mainland, each of them occupying several hundred square kilometres. The size of these and some other sea-bed basins is in part a result of the development of great ice-streams within the ice-sheet off the west coast as lesser streams emerged from confined courses in the mountains and joined together. These ice-streams were themselves restricted and deflected by the high ground of some of the islands, whose bulk was often increased by local ice accumulations. Geological factors also appear to have favoured glacial erosion of the sea bed. Relatively weak rocks beneath the Firth of Clyde help to account for its large rock basin. Glacial erosion between Jura and Colonsay was aided by the presence of Mesozoic strata on the sea bed. The vast basin between northern Skye and the mainland is probably related to sea-bed outcrops of Mesozoic rocks which, although covered by lavas in Skye, are not so protected on the mainland coast. Farther north the broad bays of Eddrachillis, Enard and Gruinard descend respectively to maximum depths of 155, 200 and 215 m yet the ice was not significantly constricted by relief. These three basins are far larger and deeper than any on the Lewisian gneiss and Torridon sandstone of the adjacent land and they may well be related to sea-bed outcrops of Mesozoic strata.

The deepest part of the sea (323 m) around the coasts of the British Isles is in the Inner Sound of Raasay and occurs in the fault-guided trench that follows the east coasts of northern Raasay and Rona. The influence of the Great Glen fault is seen in the two long narrow basins in Loch Linnhe, one of which descends to ¯220 m. The deep trench between Rhum and Eigg is probably along a major fault line and certainly relates to the con-striction of the ice flow between these islands, thus being com-parable with the basins in glacial breaches on land.

Yet bathymetry gives only an incomplete picture of the extent and depth of the sea-floor rock basins, for they contain thick accumulations of sediment. A fuller picture is provided by rock-head contour maps, such as that constructed by Binns *et al.* (1973) for the Sea of the Hebrides. The rock surface is often very irregular and in several basins lies well below ¯200 m. The most remarkable feature is a major trench some 10 km wide and 100 km long that extends southwestwards from near the island of Rhum. Along almost the whole of the trench rockhead is below ¯300 m and in one area it is below ¯380 m. The trench is almost entirely excavated in Mesozoic strata, but the relative weakness of these rocks can only partly help to explain the vast size of the feature.

Investigations with a manned submersible off the west coast of Scotland have provided visual evidence of the importance of glacial erosion on the sea floor (Eden *et al.* 1971). Smoothed and plucked rock surfaces, as well as steep rock walls of U-shaped valleys descending to flat sediment-filled floors, have been frequently observed on the sea bed. In the entrance to Loch Fyne, the longest of the Scottish fiords (70 km), a submerged rock-walled trench has been discovered along the centre of the loch. The maximum depth found in the trench was 185 m but the sediments on its floor may be as much as 150 m thick.

Most of the fiord floors of western Scotland descend seawards to depths of 100 to 200 m before the final rise at the entrance, but this descent is usually irregular, sometimes greatly so, with alternating rock bars and basins. Loch Fyne has three major basins and Loch Etive two, while Loch Sunart has at least half a dozen of varying dimensions. The fiord rock bars are sometimes largely submerged but in other instances form marked constrictions as illustrated by the names Loch Torridon, Loch Shieldaig and Upper Loch Torridon given to the three distinct parts of one fiord. The bar at the mouth of Loch Etive is so shallow that it produces a reversing tidal waterfall (the Falls of Lora). In several other instances fresh-water lochs fail to be fiords by a narrow margin. Thus the surfaces of lochs Morar and Maree are between 9 and 10 m above Ordnance Datum, Loch Lomond is about 8 m above, while Loch Hope stands less than 4 m.

On the opposite side of the country the influence of the Great Glen fault is seen in the trend of the Inverness Firth while in Inverness itself a borehole passed through almost 100 m of drift without reaching rockhead. Altogether the Great Glen fault is associated with continuous linear features for almost 200 km (including the straight coast between Inverness and Tarbat Ness), rockhead being well below sea-level over at least half this distance. Deep buried valleys have long been known in the Central Lowlands and were early interpreted as river courses. More recently George (1958) argued that the buried Kelvin valley in Glasgow was formed preglacially in relation to a sea-level approaching 90 m below present. McManus (1967) attributed the buried valley of the lower Tay, whose floor passes below –70 m, to rejuvenation caused by world sea-level lowering in glacial times, but the Tay area was covered by glacier ice when world sea-level was sufficiently low and the land was also greatly depressed isostatically.

While rivers appear to have contributed to the formation of some valleys that are now buried, such as that of the lower Tweed (p.124), there is clear evidence of glacial erosion. At the base of the steep southern slope of the western Ochils a trench parallel with the upland edge is known to descend to – 102 m (Soons 1960). At least the greater part of the trench is due to ice action for farther down the Forth valley (at Kincardine) rockhead does not fall below – 21 m. The same rock bar indicates the essentially glacial origin of a large basin cut in Old Red sandstone west of Stirling, where rockhead at – 109 m has been recorded (Francis *et al.* 1970). The deepest basin lies down valley from the Kincardine rock bar and was formed by the ice-stream that flowed through the gap between the Clyde and Forth basins south of the Kilsyth Hills. The main part of the basin is some 25 km long and is partly bounded by steep rock slopes bordering the Firth of Forth. Its deepest known point is 206 m below sea-level, whereas farther down the firth rockhead is no more than 60 m below, thus demonstrating major deepening by glacier ice (Sissons 1969). Glacial erosion along the course of the Clyde estuary is implied by the rock basin known to descend below – 70 m. Farther upstream, between Hamilton and Lanark, the Clyde flows for 13-14 km in a straight trench 100 m or more deep that contrasts sharply with the subdued relief on either side. The trench begins abruptly near Lanark, where the Clyde leaves a broad flat-floored valley to enter it by waterfalls and a vertical-sided gorge. George (1958) described the trench as an outstanding example of rejuvenation related to Tertiary lowering of sea-level but Linton (1963) interpreted it as cut by glacier ice from the Highlands that flowed up this part of the Clyde valley.

Corries

A characteristic feature of many Scottish uplands is the corrie. Exactly how many exist is uncertain and in any case depends on how the term is defined. Linton (1959) said that there are nearly 500 corries in Scotland but Godard (1965) identified 437 in the Northern Highlands and islands (including Orkney and the

Outer Hebrides). The back walls of well-developed corries vary between about 150 and 450 m in height and many corries are about a kilometre wide, although there is much variation. Less than a quarter of the corries contain lochans, many corrie floors being roughly level or sloping outwards. Rock basins are very common where rock structures dip into corries, a point well illustrated in the Applecross peninsula (Haynes 1968). In north-west Sutherland many corrie floors are formed of Lewisian gneiss and rock basins in them occur along shatter planes, especially at locations where such planes intersect (H.R. Thompson 1950). Using a sample of 72 corries from Sutherland, the Applecross area, the Cuillins, the Cairngorms and Arran, Haynes concluded that 81% of the long profiles could be fitted to a simple logarithmic curve. Simplicity is also seen in the plan of many corries whose gently curving headwalls approximate to a semicircle, well illustrated in the granite of the Cairngorms (Sugden 1969), in certain metamorphic rocks south of Braemar, and in the greywackes of the Tweedsmuir Hills.

Godard plotted corrie orientations in Scotland north of the Great Glen in terms of eight directions and found that 71% face between north and east, with the largest number facing northeast, as would be expected from climatic considerations. A plot of well defined corries in Scotland as a whole, using a much smaller number than Godard employed, revealed a preference for a north-easterly aspect but also showed that a significant proportion of corries faces north (Sissons 1967a). The latter reflects the west-east trend of many of the preglacial divides. The influence of pre-existing relief is also seen in the western Cairngorms where most corries face east or north-north-west and very few have a northeasterly aspect (Sugden 1969).

Almost 90% of the Scottish corries are concentrated in the western Highlands and adjacent islands in the area that now has more than 2250 mm precipitation (Linton 1959). Local concentrations in the eastern Grampians occur in the Cairngorms and in the high ground south of the Dee where precipitation today exceeds 1500 mm. Among corries situated farther afield are small groups in the Merrick-Kells ranges and the Tweedsmuir Hills, possibly two cut into The Cheviot (Clapperton 1970), two

in Hoy in the Orkneys, six in the island of Lewis and two in
South Uist (Godard 1965). Comparison of maps of corrie
locations by different authors reveals general agreement on broad
distribution but marked discrepancies in local detail: for example,
Robinson *et al.* (1971), although using only 'definable corrie
floor altitudes', plotted exactly twice as many corries in the
island of Lewis as did Godard.

Within small areas corrie floors show much variation in
altitude but over the country as a whole there is an eastward
increase in average altitude. For example, in the Isle of Lewis,
according to Godard's figures, all but one of the corrie floors are
between 210 and 290 m, in Skye they vary between 270 and
630 m, while in Mull all except one lie between 300 and 380 m.
On the other hand, in the heart of the Northern Highlands mid-
way between the west coast and Loch Ness corrie floors range
between 530 and 880 m. Farther east, in the western Cairngorms,
they vary between 600 and 1000 m. From Skye and Mull to the
eastern Grampians the average rise is 550-600 m in 150 km.
Farther north, as well as in southern Scotland, the eastward rise is
much less marked. In part this difference reflects the absence
from Caithness, eastern Sutherland and the central and eastern
Southern Uplands of ground high enough for the full altitudinal
range of corrie development to be represented. It also relates to
the shelter afforded to the eastern Grampians by the main
mountain mass in the west, whose effectiveness in this respect
would be enhanced in glacial times by its large ice accumulation.
Corrie floor altitudes also descend towards the Highland border
with the Central Lowlands: thus not far from the Highland edge
in Angus corries are at 500 to 700 m, including some that face
southwards, contrasting with the corries of the western Cairngorms where none are so unfavourably situated. Such differences
again suggest the importance of exposure to snow-bearing winds
and hint that in glacial times some of these winds came from a
southerly point.

In general terms the eastward increase in corrie floor altitudes,
on which is superimposed a rise towards the central Grampians
from the Highland border, indicates a similar rise in the firn line
at the times the corries were being formed. But the relationship is

far from simple. Factors such as geology, aspect and adjacent ground form may be expected to have influenced altitude. Also most or all of the corries have been submerged beneath an ice-sheet and some have been considerably modified as a consequence, especially in the southwest Grampians. Furthermore, overwhelming by external ice took place at different times in different groups of corries, so that some corries have had a much longer time than others in which to form. This point can be illustrated by reference to figure 7.5, which shows the limits of the last glacial readvance in the southeast Grampians, but which can also be taken to show glacier distributions analogous to those existing during the growth of the later ice-sheets that covered the area. It can be seen that with only modest expansion of the larger ice masses some of the small glaciers in the south and east would be overwhelmed, but that a very large accumulation of glacier ice would be needed to bury the corrie glaciers high on the northern side of Lochnagar. Such complications cause one to doubt the identifications of different generations of corries on the basis of altitude as, for example, Godard's (1965) recognition of four generations of corries each rising in altitude eastwards with the lowest group the oldest. Likewise, Sugden's (1969) recognition of three generations of corries based mainly on size, which he related to Middle Weichselian, Early Weichselian and earlier glaciations, must remain speculative, as he pointed out. Sugden's view that corries in the western Cairngorms were cut approximately to their present size before the last ice-sheet existed is partly supported in Scotland as a whole wherever moraines of the Loch Lomond Readvance (chapter 7) can be related to specific corries, by the small volume of these moraines compared with the volume of the corries.

Ice roughening and ice moulding
In addition to producing the specific features considered so far, glacier ice greatly modified the ground in many parts of Scotland, the results being seen especially in many lowlands and on some plateaux. Its effects on the Lewisian gneiss of the northwest coastlands and the Outer Hebrides have already been mentioned. The highly irregular relief of these areas, with their numerous

lochs and lochans alternating with bare rock knobs and hills was appropriately termed by Linton (1959) 'knock and lochan topo-graphy'. On the other hand, it seems inappropriate to regard this as a form of ice-moulded relief, as he did, and the term 'glacial roughening' (Sissons 1967a) seems more suitable. Roughened plateaux are extensive around Loch Ness where numerous small rock-basin lakes occur up to an altitude of 700 m. Extremely irregular rocky plateaux occur at many places in the west, up to 600 m or more above sea-level, as on either side of Loch Morar, by Loch Duich, and in the major break in the mountain belt inland from Ullapool.

In the Tweed basin the plateau between the Ettrick and Teviot rivers is strongly grained by ice that moved southwest to northeast as evidenced by numerous striae, parallel with the strike of the Silurian rocks, On either side of this area valleys aligned across the direction of ice movement are asymmetrical, with till plastered on northeast-facing slopes, while slopes facing in the opposite direction are mainly drift-free and bare rock ribs protrude from them. Farther northeast small igneous intrusions in the Old Red area form pronounced crags from which long tails taper away northeastwards. In the succeeding belt of low volcanic hills (fig. 1.5) the ice-moulded forms are imperfectly developed but on the Carboniferous sediments that follow till is often thick, and drumlins abound, ranging from long narrow features up to 7 km long (the longest recorded in the British Isles) to broader much shorter features. Towards Berwick the drumlins swing round to point eastwards and, in northern Northumberland, south of east. These trends are clearly shown on a generalised map by Clapperton (1970), although this omits an important belt of narrow northward-pointing ice-moulded forms, including excellent crag-and-tail features, some of which are shown in figure 3.4.

Most of the lower ground in the Central Lowlands has been strongly moulded by ice. In the Forth valley southeast of Stirling there are drumlins composed of thick till, including one in which a bore showed 50 m of this material. On the other hand, west of Falkirk, the ice streaming eastwards from the Clyde basin to that of the Forth produced, on a downhill gradient, a pronounced series of broad ridges and furrows that are essentially rock features veneered with drift. The Lothians and the ground between the firths of Forth and Tay are extensively ice moulded, the most common direction being E 10° N (Burke 1969). The intensity of moulding is inversely related to altitude, reflecting at least in part the greater susceptibility of the sedimentary rocks to

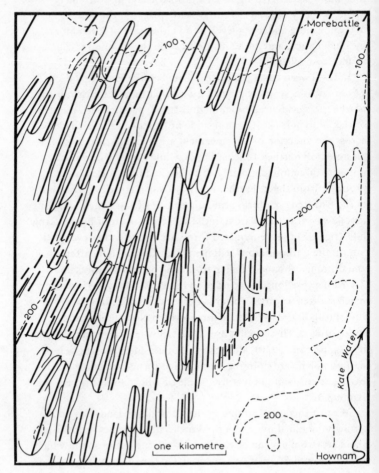

Fig. 3.4   Ice-moulded landforms west of The Cheviot. Crests of ridges denoted by heavy lines. Contour interval 100 m.

this process. Yet while the igneous rocks normally form drift-free craggy uplands and isolated hills they are usually associated with clear 'tails', composed largely or entirely of bedrock, that decline regularly in altitude eastwards. Edinburgh is classic ground in this respect. Hall (1815) introduced the term 'craig and tail' in a consideration of features such as the Castle Rock, and from striae elsewhere in the city correctly inferred that a powerful erosive agent had traversed the area in a direction E $10°$ N, although he apparently envisaged the agent as tsunamis. The crag-and-tail features are often associated with curving depressions in bedrock cut by basal ice that was forced to diverge round the crag, the depression associated with the Castle Rock being particularly marked (fig. 3.5). In central Edinburgh the depressions are partly obscured by varied superficial deposits up to 30 m thick, but very little of this material is till, implying that the features were at least partly excavated by the last ice-sheet. It may be inferred that at least 105 m of rock have been removed by ice over the deepest part of the Castle Rock depression, while adjacent to the ice-moulded cuesta of Salisbury Crags, a short distance to the east, at least 150 m of erosion by ice is indicated (Sissons 1971). Such figures are minimal since no identifiable trace of the pre-glacial relief remains. This great transformation of the land surface by ice is typical of the area on either side of the Firth of Forth. It is seen in the way most of the principal rivers for considerable distances follow ice-fashioned hollows markedly discordant to the regional slope of the land surface and to geological structures, and hence probably wholly unrelated to whatever preglacial river courses existed.

The results of glacial erosion in the area of Old Red sedimentary rocks lying between the Highland edge and the belt of volcanic hills were studied by Linton (1962). He argued that the resistant conglomerates of the Menteith Hills, which rise to over 400 m between the rivers Forth and Teith, protected the relatively weak sandstones on their immediate lee (east-south-east) side from significant glacial erosion, but with increasing distance from the hills protection became less effective. The interfluve between the two rivers tapers away over a distance of 10 km, from an initial width of 5-6 km, and over this distance falls in altitude

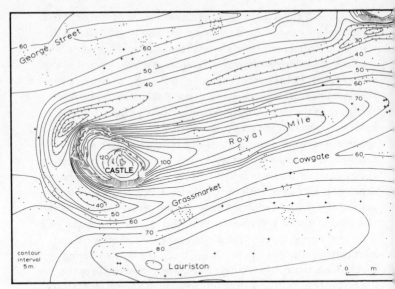

Fig. 3.5   Rockhead contours at 5 m interval in central Edinburgh. Bore-holes shown by dots and other data points by crosses.

from about 150 to 30 m. A similar 'tapered interfluve' occurs south of the river Almond. Linton also drew attention to 'bridge interfluves' exemplified by the lowland divide that separates the drainage to Loch Lomond from that to the Forth and the similar divide between the Allan and Earn drainage basins. Such inter-fluves form low but distinct barriers crossing the Old Red lowland belt from side to side. They are not related to geological controls and, although eroded by ice, are attributed to the survival of solid rock residuals in favoured locations between powerful ice-streams. From such evidence Linton suggested that (omitting the evidence of erosion below present sea-level) 100 to 120 m of rock has been removed by ice from 100 km^2 of the Forth valley and from 60 km^2 of the Earn valley.

Ice moving up the lower Clyde valley produced the drumlin field on which Glasgow is partly built. Till as much as 35 m thick has been recorded in these well-developed drumlins, which splay out through the city towards directions between east and south-east. Ice-moulded landforms are widespread in lowland Ayrshire, while on the low ground inland from the Solway Firth there are many excellent drumlins that are grouped into systems aligned in various directions. In the far north of the mainland ice flowing north to northwest across Caithness produced sharp rock ridges and grooves as it surmounted the coastal hills but over most of the area moulded the ground into broad low undulations aligned parallel with its motion (Crampton *et al.* 1914). The landforms of North Uist have been mapped by Davies (1956) who has described, in addition to a large area of irregular rocky lowland typical of the Outer Hebrides, tails of rock and till descending from hills such as Eaval and a small area of drumlins that are generally about 8 m high and 50 m long.

4 Fluvioglacial landforms

Fluvioglacial landforms, both erosional and depositional, are extensively developed in many parts of Scotland, although they are infrequent over much of the Outer Hebrides, parts of the northwestern coastal belt and in some west Highland valleys. Thousands of meltwater channels have been mapped in Scotland, typically running along hill slopes or crossing spurs, but many more have not been investigated. Fluvioglacial deposits are most common on valley floors, in basins, and on coastal lowlands, but occasionally they ascend slopes to considerable altitudes.

Meltwater channels

Most meltwater channels are small features a few metres deep and have a subdued form because they were cut in drift or because of infilling by peat or by debris that has moved down their slopes. They may form interconnected systems comprising scores of individual elements that appear as minor furrows descending gentle or moderate hill slopes obliquely, as on the flanks of Strathallan. In some areas small and large channels combine in complex systems covering areas of many square kilometres, well illustrated by the elaborate system on the flanks of Strathspey mapped by Young (1974). These channels, like many others, are associated with depositional forms. The example illustrated in figure 4.1 shows how channels and associated eskers may record various routes followed by a subglacial river system across an area.

Often the glacial river courses are recorded only intermittently, as where englacial rivers were superimposed on spur crests to become locally subglacial. Such incomplete systems are well developed on spurs adjacent to the upper Tweed (Price 1960), by

the Yarrow valley and, north of Peebles, on the eastern side of
the Eddleston valley (Sissons 1958). These various channel
systems, directed towards northeast and north, form elements of
the generally northeastward meltwater drainage pattern that
occurs over a large area extending from west of the Clyde to the
Pentland and Lammermuir hills and accords with the regional
direction of movement of Southern Uplands ice in this area. In
the lower ground of the Lothians bordering the Firth of Forth
the channels change direction to trend a little north of east
parallel with the flow of Highland ice.

Systems of exceptionally small channels are found in certain
areas covered by the Loch Lomond Readvance (chapter 7). Such
channels are best developed in the central Grampians between the
Pass of Drumochter and Glen Tilt where they are typically less
than 4 m deep, some being as little as 1 m deep and 2 m wide
(fig. 4.2). Systems of these tiny channels, comprising scores of
individual elements, show very marked difference in trend that

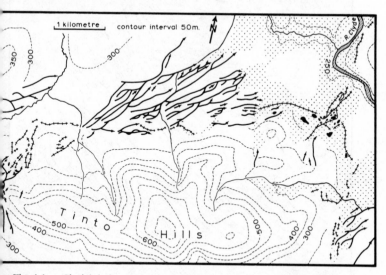

Fig. 4.1   Glacial drainage system comprising meltwater channels (arrows)
and eskers by the Tinto Hills, Lanarkshire. Kettle holes marked by solid
shading. Fluvioglacial deposits not forming kettle holes or eskers shown by
dots.

often reflect the very varied directions of flow of a local ice mass that built up during the readvance. In this they contrast with the consistent trend towards northeast and north of channels associated with (earlier) ice-sheet decay that occur over an extensive area from the flanks of the Cairngorms to the Great Glen (Sissons 1974a).

Some meltwater channels are large features 20 m or more deep and a few approach 100 m. A system of large channels in East

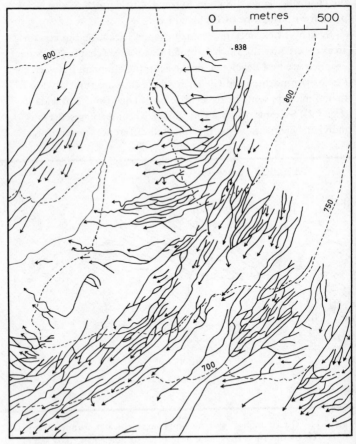

Fig. 4.2   Part of a system of very small meltwater channels on the Gaick plateau in the central Grampians. Contour interval 50 m.

Lothian extends for 30 km and gives a distinctive local character
to the terrain, trending first northeast along the fault-line scarp
and then, near Dunbar, swinging southeast with the changed
direction of the hill margin. Another series of channels, many of
them large, follows the Highland edge of the Central Lowlands
northeast of the Tay: on the hill slopes near Blairgowrie the
channels are so numerous and closely spaced that they are often
separated only by narrow ridges. Many large channels are
occupied by rivers at the present time and this has resulted in
their often being mistakenly called postglacial gorges. Various
impressive gorges in northwest Scotland may be attributed to
meltwater action, the best known being the vertical-sided Corrie-
shalloch gorge not far from Ullapool, which is a kilometre long,
60 m deep, and 25 m wide at the lip. Another, inland from Kyle
of Lochalsh, starts abruptly where the Falls of Glomach drop
through some 70 m into a vertical-walled slot a few metres wide.
That meltwaters flowed through the Killiecrankie gorge near
Pitlochry, now followed by the Perthshire Garry, is indicated by
fluvioglacial gravel spreads at its southern end. The principal river
of the Midlothian basin, the North Esk, runs in a steep-sided
channel as much as 60 m deep for 20 km, formation by meltwaters being demonstrated by large rock-cut tributary channels
drained by tiny streams and by the way in which the North Esk
near its source descends from the Pentlands to be diverted along a
large meltwater channel in which it is an obvious misfit. The meltwater gorge of the Water of Caiplich, a tributary of the Avon in
the eastern Grampians, is a striking example of glacial diversion of
drainage, which was initially attributed to river capture. Having
followed its valley in a normal manner for nearly 10 km, the
present stream suddenly turns through a right-angle to follow a
gorge 45 to 75 m deep cut clean through one side of its valley.
Beyond the abrupt bend the valley continues, at first streamless
and then occupied by a misfit stream (Linton 1954).

Gigantic semi-potholes that occur over a vertical distance of
some 60 to 90 m at one locality on the precipitous rock slope of
Glen Nevis have been interpreted as cut by water plunging down
marginal crevasses (Bailey *et al.* 1916). Near Dinnet on Deeside
an almost circular pothole some 18 m across and 12 to 18 m

deep is known as the Vat and forms part of a meltwater channel cut in granite. Another feature of some rock-cut meltwater channels is their up-and-down long profile, often attributable to subglacial formation under hydrostatic pressure. A remarkable example near Yetholm in Roxburghshire starts almost on a valley floor, climbs directly up the steep valley side through a vertical distance of more than 50 m, continues through the ridge crest and then descends through 50 m on the far side. Throughout its length of a kilometre the channel does not receive any tributaries and is cut some 10 to 15 m into rock. The up-and-down surface drift profile of a large channel in East Lothian a few kilometres from Dunbar may conceal a similar bed rock profile. It has smaller channels cut into one wall and a prominent esker on its floor. Such evidence suggests a subglacial origin and hints that some large channels have had a complicated history, probably having been formed during more than one period of ice cover. The latter is also suggested by other channels in East Lothian, some of which have thick drift on their floors or are broad features with only moderate slopes as if modified by glacial erosion. Another example from the same area is a vast channel near Gorebridge that was a major outlet for meltwaters escaping eastwards from the Midlothian basin. For a considerable distance the channel is a simple clear-cut feature several hundred metres broad but it is then almost completely blocked by a great mass of fluvioglacial material. Complete obliteration of some meltwater channels in Midlothian is suggested by borehole evidence that has revealed buried valleys whose trend points to a meltwater origin (Tulloch and Walton 1958).

Of larger dimensions is the completely buried trench that underlies the lower Carron at Falkirk and trends slightly north of east through Grangemouth to merge into the deep rock basin that underlies the Forth. While erosion by glacier ice of the latter is implied by its form and size (p. 51), the Carron trench is less easily explained in this way, for it is only about a kilometre wide and has steep sides that descend in the deepest known part to more than 80 m below sea-level. Bores show that there is no till in the trench, proving it to be infilled with sand up to 45 m thick (which is overlain by till and marine deposits). This evidence

strongly suggests that the feature was largely formed by a subglacial river. The Carron trench is only part of a buried trench
that extends for 80 km across the waist of Scotland from the
Clyde estuary to the Firth of Forth with dimensions comparable
to the tunneldale of eastern Denmark and the Rinnentäler of
northern Germany. It appears probable that in its narrower parts
this trench represents the course of a major meltwater river,
probably flowing at very considerable depth below the ice surface, but that in its wider and deeper parts (as beneath the Firth
of Forth) glacial erosion was of great importance (Sissons 1969).

A buried channel along the course of the upper Nith was
identified by Lumsden and Davies (1965). They traced it for
8 km down valley to the vicinity of New Cumnock, after which
there is a lack of borehole evidence for 5-6 km on either side of
the Southern Uplands fault, and then mapped it for a further
9 km to Sanquhar. The channel is normally a few hundred metres
across, although it widens to a kilometre around New Cumnock.
The channel fill is up to 53 m deep and consists mainly of water-
sorted deposits varying in thickness up to 40 m overlain by till
as much as 20 m thick. Lumsden and Davies dismiss glacial
erosion as the cause of the buried feature and conclude that it is a
preglacial river valley. Furthermore, since the floor of the buried
channel slopes eastwards where borehole data are available, but in
the intervening gap across the Southern Uplands fault must rise
eastwards to link the two identified parts of the channel floor, it
is inferred that movement of the fault, with downthrow to the
northwest of 50-60 m, occurred late in the history of the river
system but before the last glaciation of the area. This important
inference is very questionable, however, and the authors gave no
consideration to the likely explanation that the buried channel
was essentially cut by a major subglacial river.

Fluvioglacial depositional forms
Many valleys in the central and eastern Grampians contain large
accumulations of fluvioglacial deposits disposed as terraces and
mounds that flank the lower valley slopes and occupy the valley
floors except where destroyed along the present river courses.
The most extensive deposits are in Strathspey, where they extend

for tens of kilometres and include broad terraced outwash plains, complex esker systems, and lake-filled kettle holes such as Vaa, Roid, Garten and Mallachie. Southeast and south of Aviemore the deposits blanket the slopes of the Cairngorms up to an altitude of 600 m or so. In nearby Glen Feshie series of north-ward-sloping kame terraces and outwash terraces that rise as much as 40 m above the present river have been accurately levelled by Young (in the press). Many other valleys contain terraces that have not yet been studied in detail, such as the excellent suite cut into the mass of outwash that occupies the valley of the lower Findhorn. South of the Cairngorms, Glen Luibeg contains large kames and associated forms developed in relation to an englacial water-table at slightly over 500 m altitude that was controlled by a large rock-cut meltwater channel. Kame-and-kettle topography and eskers are well developed in valleys tributary to the Dee south of Balmoral while farther east in Dee-side the massive outwash spreads at Dinnet have long been known. Terraces on the slopes of the Tummel-Tay valley extending past Pitlochry to Dunkeld were variously explained as marine shore-lines, ice-dammed lake shorelines and river terraces, but Bremner (1939) re-interpreted them as kame terraces. Some of these terraces are composed of coarse gravel laid down by proglacial or marginal rivers, but others are composed of silt and fine sand and may have accumulated in narrow marginal lakes related to an englacial water-table.

The outwash terraces and meltwater channels that lead from the southwest end of Loch Awe towards the coast are particularly interesting since they show that the loch once drained that way, its present outlet being near its head through the fault-guided glacial breach of the Pass of Brander to Loch Etive. Outwash deposits occur in several westward-draining valleys between lochs Awe and Etive, but are most impressive near Loch Etive, the entrance to which is greatly constricted by a large, kettled west-ward-sloping mass of outwash (fig. 7.3). Conspicuous kettled terraces that border the loch east of the outwash were considered by McCann (1961, 1966a) to have been laid down in ice-marginal lakes, but detailed levelling by Gray (1972) showed that they have pronounced westward gradients which, along with their usually coarse composition, show that they are essentially river-deposited kame terraces.

Farther north on the west coast a large kettled outwash mass greatly constricts Loch Linnhe at Corran while another conspicuous mass lies at the entrance to Loch Carron. In the centre of the Northern Highlands at Achnasheen a suite of large outwash terraces slopes down eastwards; west of the hamlet the terraced deposits divide to follow separate valleys in each of which, after a short distance, they terminate abruptly in ice-contact slopes making former positions of the edge of the ice-sheet. Outwash spreads and eskers are well developed alongside and near the Dornoch and Cromarty firths, the outwash spreads in some instances being closely linked to former changes of sea-level. One of the most massive eskers in Scotland in the entrance to the Great Glen near Inverness is currently being destroyed by gravel workings. Farther east, an esker system extends for 8 km near Nairn and flattish-topped spreads of fluvioglacial deposits pitted with dead-ice hollows occur at Elgin, while on the slopes of the rising ground to the south of Nairn series of kame terraces decline gently north-eastwards for many kilometres.

The thickness of fluvioglacial deposits appears to be considerable in parts of the Highlands, especially beneath valley floors. Sections high on the flanks of the Cairngorms reveal 60 m, sections by the Spey expose a similar thickness (along with other deposits) and borehole data in Inverness indicate at least 90 m of sand and gravel in one locality. Such bores as exist in fluvioglacial deposits in Highland valleys often fail to reach rockhead but the steepness of valley sides plunging beneath the deposits is suggestive. Interesting detail is available from Glen Tromie, tributary to the Spey. Here as much as 75 m of fluvioglacial and 'morainic' deposits occur. Tunnelling operations in the drift revealed cavities up to about 4 m across, which appear to mark the positions of buried blocks of ice, total collapse having been prevented owing to the coarseness of the material (J.G.C. Anderson 1951).

Fluvioglacial deposits are extensive on the Old Red lowland belt bordering the Highlands on the south. The floor of Strathallan is covered with kames and dead-ice hollows, some of the debris having been supplied by meltwater channels cut into the surrounding slopes. Strathearn, and the Tay valley near Perth, contain large outwash spreads. In western Strathmore the surfaces of massive flat-topped accumulations of sand separated by broad dead-ice hollows, as well as kame terraces and the tops of kame ridges, have been shown by accurate measurement to integrate into a gentle eastward slope over a distance of 25 km. Deposition by eastward-flowing rivers of an extensive sand plain around large masses of dead ice is indicated. The meltwaters escaped into eastern Strathmore through a major meltwater channel located near Forfar. Later meltwater flow southwards is demonstrated by a pitted outwash plain with an area of 20 km^2 that slopes radially outwards from Blairgowrie at the Highland edge and merges into the outwash terraces of the Tay valley (E.V. Insch, unpublished). The vast outwash plain is composed of coarse gravel near Blairgowrie, where remains of the complex braided stream system that formed it can be clearly seen, grading into sand towards its outer parts. Another extensive outwash mass, which leads out from the Highland edge near Edzell in eastern Strathmore, has been cut into a series of terraces by the North Esk and West Water. The braided channels on the highest terrace are so pronounced in one locality that the rises between them resemble low kames.

On the opposite side of the Central Lowlands kames and kettles are almost continuous in a belt along the border with the Southern Uplands from the east coast to beyond the Clyde and were interpreted by Charlesworth (1926) as part of his Lammermuir-Stranraer kame moraine, here supposed to have been formed along the margin of Highland ice. They are dead-ice features, however, and most of them were laid down amidst Southern Uplands ice, as for example, in the Eddleston valley (which drains south to join the Tweed at Peebles), where meltwater drainage to the south was initially prevented by the decaying Southern Uplands ice. Meltwaters had to escape from the northern end of the valley, resulting in the development of an englacial water-table in the dead ice, meltwater channels being cut above the level of the water-table and kames and kettles being deposited below it, while at its level kame terraces accumulated. The water-table was drained when meltwater flow to the south beneath the ice was established, as evidenced by a meltwater channel cut deep into rock that descends almost to the floor of the Eddleston valley (Sissons 1958).

A similar reversal of drainage associated with the decay of Southern Uplands ice occurred in the West Linton basin at the foot of the Pentland Hills. The accumulation of a complex of kames and kettles in the basin was related to an englacial water-table controlled by a meltwater channel leading northwards to the North Esk and ultimately to the Firth of Forth. The estab-lishment of southward drainage to the Tweed while dead ice still occupied the basin is demonstrated by a meltwater channel that, cut deeply into the kame-and-kettle topography, feeds into a long sinuous esker on the floor of the basin.

The Carstairs ridge system in the Clyde valley, which extends for 10 km and consists of ridges up to 25 m high separated by elongated kettle holes, has caused much dispute. Composed mainly of sand and gravel, but including great quantities of partly-rounded boulders up to a metre across, it was interpreted by Charlesworth (1926) as formed along the margin of Highland ice and by Goodlet (1964) as a moraine produced along the margin of Southern Uplands ice. However, McLellan (1969) stated that the deposits are entirely water-laid and from the form of the features and measurements of stratification and imbrica-tion concluded that they are an esker system.

The terraces of the North Esk in Midlothian have been studied in detail by Kirby (1969a), who mapped 175 terrace remnants, most of them outwash, and obtained 1200 altitudes on them by accurate levelling. Deposition occurred because the Esk, carrying debris north-eastwards from decaying Southern Uplands ice, found its course blocked by ice wasting back towards the Firth of Forth. Each of the eleven outwash terraces identified by Kirby is lower and ex-tends farther north-eastwards than its predecessor, each ends in an ice-contact slope, and the lower end of each (excepting one) corre-lates in altitude with a channel to the east that carried meltwaters out of the area. A complication is introduced, however, in that four of the terraces, according to Kirby, are covered by till (the Roslin Till) laid down during a minor readvance of the northern ice. A detailed study of the Tweed terraces has been made by Rhind (1969) who obtained about 11,000 levelled altitudes. Many of the terrace remnants cannot be justifiably correlated over more than a short distance, but the general pattern is of a succession of terraces most of which rise up valley for a limited distance. Some terraces end up valley in kame-and-kettle topography that extends below their level, implying formation immediately downstream from decaying ice, and the pattern as a whole reflects ice decay towards the high ground of the central Southern Uplands with the Tweed as the major route for escaping meltwaters.

Ice-dammed lakes

Many ice-dammed lakes have been claimed to have existed in Scotland based largely or entirely on the assumption that melt-water channels are lake overflow channels (e.g. Charlesworth 1955; J.G.C. Anderson and Dunham 1966). Without depositional evidence such claims must be rejected. Such evidence for a former lake in part of the Spey valley was cited by Bremner (1934), who described extensive accumulations of sand and silt up to 60 m thick that occur around Rothes and Knockando. The lake is believed to have been held up by the Moray Firth ice mass, debris being poured into it from ice that had come down the Spey valley. The sediments have been cut into a series of excellent terraces interpreted by Bremner as related to overflow channels that carried the escaping lake waters eastwards past the site of Keith.

Laminated (probably varved) sediments related to small ice-dammed lakes are known from various localities in Scotland and a few short stretches of lake shoreline have been identified at scattered points. In only two areas have shorelines been extensively identified however. One of these areas is Rannoch Moor, in the western Grampians, where Mathieson and Bailey (1925) mapped shorelines at several levels. Accurate levelling shows that some, at least, of these features are essentially horizontal (K.S.R. Thompson 1972).

The 'parallel roads' of glens Roy, Gloy and Spean are by far the most remarkable shorelines of former lakes in the British Isles. Numerous papers have been written about them and a variety of interpretations put forward but L. Agassiz' early

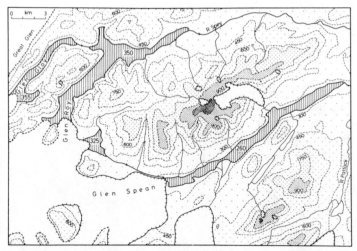

Fig. 4.3   Ice-dammed lakes in glens Roy, Gloy and Spean at the maximum of the Loch Lomond Readvance. Contour interval 150 m.

suggestion greatly elaborated by Jamieson (1863) remains substantially correct. A readvance of ice blocked the three glens to produce lakes at 355 m in Glen Gloy, 350 m in Glen Roy and 260 m in Glen Spean, each lake overflowing through a col (fig. 4.3). The Roy lake at this time was about 16 km long and as much as 200 m deep. Ice decay enabled lower escape routes to be used by the Roy lake, which fell to 325 and then to 260 m, the three shorelines (and, in places, a faint fourth one unrelated to a col) forming the famous 'parallel roads'. The last 'road', at the same level in glens Roy and Spean, is associated with conspicuous deltas and deltaic fans outside the glacial readvance limit. This 'road' also occurs for many kilometres inside the limit, although it is missing where glacier tongues that had descended from the Ben Nevis range were wasting away. North of Loch Treig the ground above the 'road' is often bare rock, but below and at the level of the 'road' extensive fluvioglacial deposits are disposed as steep-sided ridges separated by deep kettles, some of the former running into the 'road' (fig. 7.2). This evidence indicates that here the 'road' is a kame terrace and implies that the open lake was in places continued through the decaying ice as an englacial water-table (Sissons 1967a). At its greatest extent the water body had a length of about 35 km. Its final drainage and that of the Glen Gloy lake was through the Great Glen north-eastwards to the Moray Firth. The river that drains Glen Gloy abruptly abandons its clear former valley, bending north-westwards through more than 90 degrees in a gorge, probably of subglacial origin, that cuts through the old valley side. The Spean, which also bends north-westwards through a gorge to abandon its former valley, is followed by a suite of large terraces that decline towards the Great Glen.

5 Ice extent and thickness

At its greatest extent the ice-sheet that covered Scotland terminated in the sea beyond the Outer Hebrides. That the ice-sheet
covered the distant island of North Rona (70 km northwest of
Cape Wrath) is shown by Torridonian and Cambrian-Ordovician
erratics, while erratics have also been reported from Sula Sgeir
20 km farther west. Erratics also occur on the Flannan Islands
(30 km west of Harris) but they appear to be absent from St
Kilda (70 km west of the Outer Hebrides), suggesting that the ice
failed to reach here.

In the east the Scottish ice appears to have been confluent
with the Scandinavian ice, for the great ice-stream that flowed
eastwards and northeastwards into the Moray Firth suffered
marked deflection. Part of the ice-stream moved back onto the
southern coastlands, this being demonstrated by till containing
marine shells and Mesozoic erratics derived from the floor of the
Moray Firth, but a major part turned to flow north and northwest across Caithness, this being proved by ice-moulding and
striae, as well as by marine shells and erratics. Among the erratics
is the remarkable Leavad erratic of Cretaceous sandstone
measuring 220 by 140 by 8 m that rests on shelly marine clay at
least 8 m thick, the whole having been carried at least 15 km
(Crampton *et al.* 1914). Striae generally point northwestwards in
the Orkney Islands and shelly till is widespread except in the high
ground of Hoy.

Evidence relating to the thickness of the ice-sheet is available
from many areas of high ground. Striae have been observed up to
an altitude of almost 900 m in the mountains of northwest
Scotland, while erratics have been found on or near various
summits up to an altitude of 980 m. Striae have been recorded at

1100 m on the summit ridge of Aonach Beag in the Ben Nevis range and granite erratics have been seen at a similar altitude near Glencoe. Erratics of Rannoch granite reach 1060 m on Schiehallion in the central Grampians, while between the Loch Garry and Loch Ericht glacial breaches they are very common up to the highest summit at over 1000 m. Granite erratics carried eastwards from the Cairngorms are said to lie on the summit of Morven (872 m). Striae occur at over 900 m on Ben Vorlich near the Highland edge in Perthshire, striated stones have been reported from the highest ground of the Ochils (720 m), and erratics have been found on the highest point in the Pentland Hills. On Merrick (842 m), the culminating point of the Southern Uplands, granite erratics from the adjacent Loch Doon intrusion are common. Such evidence suggests that much or all of Scotland south of the Highlands was covered by ice and that only the highest parts of the Highlands could have stood above the ice surface. Yet such evidence gives only minimal altitudes. The distance the Scottish ice extended southwards in the Irish Sea and its vicinity (along with the altitude it reached in North Wales) implies that in its heart area the surface of the Scottish ice-sheet stood above the highest mountain summits. That the ice-sheet stood very far above may seem to be implied by the calculations of the dimensions of ideal ice-sheets made by physicists, but it was not of simple ideal form.

It consisted of a series of domes of varying importance whose interaction with each other has contributed to the difficulties of establishing the glacial sequence (fig. 5.1). The great importance of the major ice dome in the southwest Grampians, centred in the Rannoch basin and its vicinity, is attested by the radiating valleys and associated breaches and also by the collectively radial distribution of granite erratics. Erratics from the Glen Fyne outcrop occur around Loch Lomond, in the Strathblane glacial breach and on the Kilpatrick Hills and were also carried into the Clyde basin. The Etive granite erratics were transported southwest and especially west, for they abound in the Oban area. Rannoch granite was taken east down the Rannoch valley and also northeast into Strathspey (fig. 3.1).

The elongated major ice dome of the Northern Highlands, its

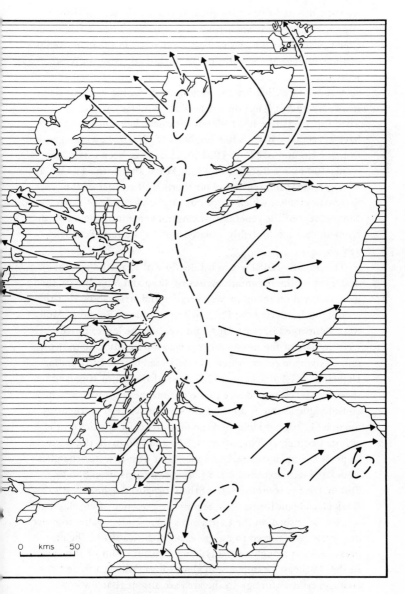

Fig. 5.1   Scottish ice domes and some major directions of ice-sheet flow.

ice-shed situated east of the present watershed, was probably composed of several smaller culminations but a broad radial outflow towards northwest and west is reflected in the main trends of the sea lochs and is indicated by high-level striae. In Wester Ross erratics carried towards the coast hint strongly that the ice surface stood well above the mountains for some were moved markedly up hill. Thus on An Teallach boulders of 'thrust' Torridon sandstone lie at 900 m although their source cannot have exceeded 450 m, while boulders of 'thrust' Lewisian gneiss near the summit of Slioch (981 m) must have been carried upwards 300 m in a distance of 4 km (Peach and Horne 1913b). In Morvern, Ardnamurchan and northern Mull erratics of the Strontian granite, which crops out on the west side of Loch Linnhe, record the general westward movement of the ice-sheet from an ice-shed probably situated well to the east (Peacock 1970).

The broadly radial westward outflow of Highland ice was deflected by the mountain masses of Skye and Mull and by the ice nourished on them. In Mull erratics and striae show that the mountains bordering the Firth of Lorne and the Sound of Mull were submerged beneath Highland ice, but the less exposed western part of the mountain area was apparently able to maintain its own ice cover, which was deflected by the surrounding Highland ice (Bailey *et al.* 1924). East of the major Highland ice-shed there is clear evidence that ice from the southwest reached considerable altitudes on the flanks of the western Cairngorms. Sugden (1970) has identified the limit of schist erratics on the granite bedrock as lying between 840 and 760 m on the northern slope of the uplands, and the upper limit of meltwater channels associated with external ice as falling eastwards from 885 to 760 m. On the southern side of the Cairngorms schist erratics and fluvioglacial landforms again record the presence of enveloping ice. Ice nourished on the Cairngorms themselves, unable to move out freely, was forced to escape east-north-eastwards, the impressive Avon trough probably being a major result of this flow. In the southeast Grampians, in glens Clova, Muick, Esk and vicinity, erratics foreign to the area are absent (Barrow *et al.* 1912) and local ice prevailed, although on the border with Strathmore ice nourished farther to the west was more powerful and carried Old Red erratics as much as 6 km north of the Highland Fault.

In lowland Ayrshire shelly drift with Highland erratics is widespread, deposited by ice from the great stream that moved down the Firth of Clyde from the southwest Grampians. The shelly drift has been found in part of this area at altitudes up to 300 m and has been reported to exceed 400 m not far from Muirkirk. Yet south of a line passing close to Cumnock and Maybole it is absent, even in much lower ground, and drift from the Southern Uplands characterised by Loch Doon granite erratics occurs. The shelly drift has also been found in a narrow strip along the coast of southern Ayrshire and more widely over the Stranraer peninsula, erratics from the island of Ailsa Craig also being common around this town. It thus appears that over the western Southern Uplands there existed an ice dome which, aided by the bulk of the upland mass, was sufficiently powerful to fend off the great Highland ice stream. Erratics from the several granite masses show the broad pattern of movement of the Southern Uplands ice. Unable to move far to the north and west, it flowed partly southwards, but especially east and northeast, as shown by the widespread moulding of the Ettrick-Teviot-Tweed area and by the meltwater drainage alignment from the Clyde area to the Lammermuirs. Opinions have varied as to whether the high ground culminating in The Cheviot remained ice free, but Clapperton (1970) has argued from the evidence of glacial drift, meltwater channels and certain glacial erosion forms that a local ice dome existed here.

The various ice movements described above do not necessarily refer to times of maximal glaciation. Thus it may be that Mull, located close to the major ice dome of the western Highlands, was completely overwhelmed by Highland ice during maximal glaciation, and that the sanctuary free from Highland erratics identified by Bailey *et al.* (1924) relates to a later phase. However, this type of argument carries less weight with increasing distance from the major western ice centres. Thus the absence of erratics in the area around The Cheviot could well relate to maximal ice cover. This interpretation is supported by the northward-directed ice-moulded landforms, many of which, being partly or wholly fashioned in bedrock, are difficult to reconcile with major ice movement from any other direction (fig. 3.4). That the south-east Grampians were never overwhelmed by external ice seems to be implied not only by the lack of foreign erratics but also by the absence of major glacial breaches. In the western Cairngorms the lack of metamorphic erratics on much of the granite points to a similar conclusion. The apparent inability of the powerful western ice to cover these areas of high ground in the east places restrictions on the maximal surface altitude that may be invoked for its highest part. An exact figure cannot be given but a maximal altitude of around 1500 m seems a reasonable estimate.

6   Quaternary events before the Loch Lomond Readvance

Very little is known about the sequence of Quaternary events in Scotland before the last ice-sheet began to decay. The evidence for interglacials in East Anglia and the English Midlands shows that Scotland was covered by ice-sheets on several occasions, but only two interglacial sites are yet known. Glaciers in Scotland were dominantly erosive and the evidence for earlier glaciations was normally destroyed during later ones. The major erosional features by virtue of their dimensions point to prolonged glacial action but do not provide a basis for establishing a sequence of events.

Various workers have used evidence such as till sheets and landform assemblages in attempts to determine successive late-Quaternary events, and especially to determine the limits of readvances that were supposed to have interrupted the decay of the last ice-sheet. Most of the interpretations that have been proposed have been shown to be unsatisfactory in one or more respects. In this chapter some of the basic evidence will be considered and various interpretations and the reasons for dismissing them will be discussed.

Interglacial sites

It is only quite recently that interglacial sites have been found in Scotland, both of them in Shetland. At Fugla Ness in the extreme north of Mainland peat up to 1.4 m thick is covered by and rests upon glacial till. Pollen and macroscopic plant remains indicate the former existence of open coniferous woodland, alternating with heath and grassland communities, developed on heavily podsolised soils. A climate warmer than that of today, with mild frost-free winters, is inferred, but climatic deterioration is indicated in the upper part of the peat. The organic deposits are tentatively correlated with the Hoxnian interglacial of East Anglia (Birks and Ransom 1969). The other interglacial site, also possibly of Hoxnian age, is on the Walls peninsula and comprises almost half a metre of peat covered by glacial deposits (Birks, unpublished).

The interglacial age of the peats places them beyond the range of radiocarbon dating, yet four finite radiocarbon dates have been obtained for them. The Fugla Ness peat has given dates of 34,800 (+900, −800), 37,000 (+1200, −1100) and 40,000 (+2000, −1600) B.P. while the Walls peat has yielded a date of 36,800 (+1950, −1560) B.P. Along with anomalous dates obtained for some English interglacial deposits, these dates are generally considered to reflect contamination and are therefore rejected (except by Page (1972)). They are important, however, since they imply that other 'old' radiocarbon dates for which an infinite value was not anticipated (e.g. some of those mentioned below) may also be greatly in error.

Northeast Scotland

The fullest evidence relating to Quaternary events in Scotland comes from the northeast, well away from the major ice centres, and has been investigated for more than a century, initially especially by Jamieson and later particularly by Bremner and Synge. The most discussed section is at the Bay of Nigg close to Aberdeen and shows sand and gravel containing Scandinavian erratics and erratics from north of Aberdeen, overlain by grey till containing Highland stones, this merging upwards into red till with Old Red erratics. Using this section and much additional evidence Synge (1956, 1963) inferred that Scandinavian ice invaded the Aberdeen area from the east or northeast and was followed by Scottish ice from the north and northwest. These events were assigned to the penultimate glaciation. Synge considered that during the last glaciation ice from the Highlands moved down the Dee valley to reach the coast, but that it was later pushed aside by ice that deposited the red till, the latter ice mass having previously flowed over Strathmore. The Strathmore ice was considered to have extended northwards to the vicinity of Peterhead, its marginal part covering a coastal strip where red deposits now occur. Near Peterhead these red deposits were said to interdigitate with shelly drift containing Jurassic erratics that extends through the coastal belt of northern Aberdeenshire and Banffshire and was deposited by ice that had passed over the bed of the Moray Firth. Synge concluded that when the two ice masses were confluent some 2000 km^2 of northeast Scotland remained ice-free but completely surrounded by ice (fig. 6.1), a conclusion reached independently by Charlesworth (1955). Synge claimed that this ice-free enclave has suffered more intense weathering than the surrounding area and referred to periglacially-smoothed slopes, highly-shattered bedrock, deeply-oxidised till and deeply-weathered igneous rock within it. He argued that this area has not been ice-covered since the last interglacial, when the chemical weathering probably occurred, and was later subjected to intense periglacial processes when surrounded by glacier ice.

Fitzpatrick (1963, 1972) accepted the concept of an ice-free enclave and the view that the till in this area is more weathered than that of the surrounding ground. He stated, however, that the bedrock is much more weathered than the till above it, and attributed this weathering to Tertiary times. A radiocarbon date of 28,100 (+480, −450) for a fossil podsol at Teindland (a few kilometres west of the lower Spey) was stated by Fitzpatrick (1965) to be minimal since alkali pretreatment could not be carried out. He suggested that the fossil soil developed as a result of long and continuous leaching during the last interglacial period and interpreted the 2 m of overlying material as till and outwash gravel. Romans *et al.* (1966) preferred to regard the material overlying the dated soil as a solifluction deposit, implying that this locality, along with a large area in northeast Scotland, was not covered by the last Scottish ice-sheet.

Since no interglacial deposits have yet been found interbedded with the till sheets of northeast Scotland there is no firm evidence that the sequence dates back beyond the last glaciation. If a large area remained unglaciated during the last glaciation interglacial peat might be expected to survive in suitable locations beneath

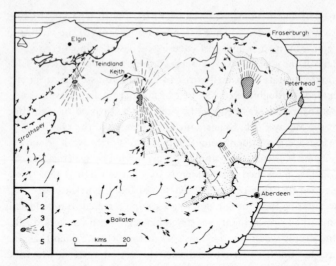

Fig. 6.1   Glacial limits and some glacial evidence in northeast Scotland based almost entirely on Synge (1956). 1. Ice limits according to Synge. 2. Limit of Elgin oscillation according to Peacock *et al.* (1968). 3. Meltwater channels. 4. Erratic trains. 5. Limit of unglaciated enclave.

soliflucted material, but such peat has not been found. On the other hand, peat beneath 60-90 cm of solifluction debris at the base of a short slope has been dated at 12,200±170 B.P., proving that some, at least, of the periglacial activity relates to lateglacial times. Furthermore, there is no firm evidence showing that the so-called ice-free enclave has suffered more severely from periglacial processes than the surrounding ground. In fact, C.M. Clapperton and D.E. Sugden (unpublished) consider that the whole of northeast Scotland was covered by the last ice-sheet. Clear meltwater channel systems are of widespread occurrence in Buchan and related ice-contact fluvioglacial landforms occupy many valleys and embayments. These features indicate ice-sheet downwastage and recession from a node where three separate ice-streams were confluent.

Midlothian
Two till sheets have long been known from part of the Midlothian basin south of Edinburgh. Three are now recognised as a result of

detailed studies by Kirby (1968, 1969b) involving stratigraphy, 64 till fabric analyses, and stone counts of a total of 7500 particles taken from till at 36 sites. A grey basal till containing very little greywacke was deposited by ice that moved due east despite the obstacle provided by the Pentland Hills. This till grades upwards into grey fluvioglacial deposits, sometimes several metres thick, that are abruptly succeeded by a red-brown till with a high proportion of greywacke brought by Southern Uplands ice moving northeast and north. The red-brown till also grades upwards into fluvioglacial deposits, these exceeding 20 m in thickness. The top till (Roslin Till) has a low greywacke content and was deposited by Highland ice that, curving round the northern end of the Pentland Hills, pushed southwards into the Midlothian basin to the vicinity of Penicuik. Fossil frost wedges occur in the fluvioglacial sands that underlie this last till sheet, implying a glacial readvance, possibly only local, which was related by Kirby to the North Esk terrace sequence (p. 69). No organic materials that could help to date the Midlothian basin deposits are known.

Some early radiocarbon dates

Evidence for ice movements very different in direction from the latest movements is available from two points on the east coast. Some 35 to 40 km south of Aberdeen, around Inverbervie and Benholm, shelly till, Mesozoic erratics and Aberdeenshire igneous rocks indicate ice flow almost directly opposed to the later movement of Strathmore ice. At Berwick marine shells from sand and gravel and overlying till that have been dated as more than 41,100 radiocarbon years old indicate ice flow quite different from that responsible for the ice-moulding of this part of the Tweed basin. The date for the shells leaves uncertain the time they were deposited: they may be related to very early ice movement, but it is also possible that they were deposited by the last ice-sheet, ice emanating from the Central Lowlands having curved round to flow back onto the land before being replaced by Tweed ice. Uncertainty likewise attaches to the time of deposition of ice-transported marine shells from Banffshire dated as more than 39,500 radiocarbon years old and from Caithness as more than 40,800.

A radiocarbon date of 27,550 (+1370, –1680) B.P. was
obtained for a woolly rhinoceros bone found in fluvioglacial
gravels beneath till at Bishopbriggs near Glasgow (Rolfe 1966),
while peat beneath material interpreted as till at Tolsta Head in
Lewis gave a date of 27,333 ±240 (von Weymarn and Edwards
1973). Along with the date of 28,100 (+480, –450) from
Teindland in Morayshire, these dates, if valid, indicate that much
of Scotland was ice-free at this time. The Bishopbriggs date is
particularly significant for the site is only a limited distance from
the greatest area of ice accumulation in the British Isles. It is
therefore possible that the whole country was ice-free. Probably
around 25,000 radiocarbon years ago the last ice-sheet began to
build up, to reach its greatest extent some 17,000-18,000 years
ago.

Supposed readvances of the last ice-sheet

From time to time during the last half century various workers
have proposed limits for readvances that are believed to have
interrupted the decay of the last ice-sheet. The first to do so was
Charlesworth (1926), who described the Lammermuir-Stranraer
kame moraine. From East Lothian to the vicinity of the Clyde
this feature was said to mark the limit of Highland ice, but farther
west this ice was said to have been confluent with Southern
Uplands ice. The southern limit of the latter was considered to be
recorded by abundant fluvioglacial deposits in the Stranraer area,
by a line separating earlier drumlins pointing south-west from a
later set directed south-south-east near Wigtown Bay, and by the
large fluvioglacial accumulations in the Dumfries basin. Evidence
of ice readvance to the supposed limit is lacking, however, and, as
indicated on p. 68 and by Kirby's evidence (p. 83), much of
the area supposed to have been last occupied by Highland ice was
in fact last covered by Southern Uplands ice.

Charlesworth (1955) also published an extensive study of the
Highlands and islands based on his own field work and that of
others, especially Geological Survey work. He identified two
major ice limits and twenty minor ones, but only occasionally do
his limits bear any relation to identifiable features that can be
reasonably interpreted as indicating former ice-margin positions.

His major correlations were dependent on the so-called '100-foot' and '50-foot' raised beaches, which do not exist.

Synge (1956, 1963) concluded that, after the Strathmore ice had wasted away, ice advanced down the Dee valley to occupy the Aberdeen area (fig. 6.1). However, S. Simpson (1948, 1955) found that the deposits of the Strathmore and Dee ice masses are intimately related to each other and inferred that both ice masses last occupied the area contemporaneously. Clapperton and Sugden (1972) obtained similar evidence and also pointed out that fluvioglacial systems are not in accord with the supposed readvance limit. Synge correlated his Aberdeen Readvance with a readvance of Moray Firth ice to the mouth of the Spey, claiming that there is here a significant line between two types of surface drift. Peacock *et al.* (1968) were unable to confirm this line but claimed to identify a readvance limit in the same general area over a distance of 35 km. The evidence for this readvance is also unconvincing, however: the mapped limit is based mainly on fluvioglacial forms and the apparent absence of fossil frost wedges within the limit was considered significant. Such wedges are now known at various places well within the supposed limit.

The present author proposed three readvances: the Aberdeen-Lammermuir, Perth and Loch Lomond readvances. The first two must now be rejected but there is abundant evidence for the last, which is considered separately in chapter 7. The evidence around Aberdeen discussed above is inconsistent with a so-called Aberdeen-Lammermuir Readvance in that area. In the Lammermuirs the readvance limit was based on fluvioglacial forms, but these do not prove a readvance. In the Tweed basin the limit was placed close to the lower Tweed but detailed mapping of the drumlins by the author shows that they cross the supposed limit in complete disregard of it.

The Perth Readvance was first described by J.B. Simpson (1933). In the lower Earn and Tay valleys extensive outwash deposits can be seen in places to overlie raised marine sediments. The most significant area is northwest of Perth where a large outwash spread rises up valley to become pitted with deep kettle holes at Almondbank. A section shows the outwash resting on rhythmically-bedded marine sediments, which in turn rest on till.

Simpson considered the rhythmites to be varves and estimated that they took 640 years to accumulate. This in turn seemed to imply a prolonged halt in ice-margin retreat in the vicinity of Almondbank or, more probably, a readvance of the ice to that locality. However, Paterson (1974) argued that the rhythmites are not annual deposits but represent successive discharges of sediment down the front of an advancing delta. On this interpretation many layers may have been deposited in a single year and the whole marine sequence may therefore have accumulated in a short time, the overlying gravels having been laid down as the outwash delta built out into the sea. Paterson also found that the widespread fluvioglacial landforms of western Strathmore provide no evidence for a major readvance, a view supported by the detailed work of E.V. Insch (unpublished).

The evidence for glacial readvance in the Clyde basin and in Ayrshire is considerable. The movement of Highland ice up the Clyde valley recorded by drumlins splaying out east and southeast through Glasgow resulted in the formation of an ice-dammed lake, which was gradually extinguished as the ice advanced. The lake is recorded by beds of clay, silt and sand, in places over 30 m thick, that are covered by till. In some localities these stratified deposits are contorted and in others they contain fossil frost wedges beneath the overlying till. In places they occupy steep-sided, river-cut buried valleys as much as 90 m deep which, lacking any till beneath the stratified deposits (it occurs beneath these deposits elsewhere), must have been cut (or at least cleaned out) before the ice readvanced. A few marine shells, whose authenticity has been questioned, were found long ago in deposits associated with the readvance. More significant is J. Wright's (1896) examination of ten till samples from the Glasgow area, in all of which he found foraminifers, thus implying that the sea penetrated the Clyde estuary before the readvance. Remains of mammoth, woolly rhinoceros and reindeer have been found in the till of the Clyde basin or in the underlying stratified deposits. In the Airdrie area wisps of peat in till contained a species of Arctic willow along with beetles that at present have a pronounced northern distribution (Bennie 1896; Coope 1962). From the same area A. Geikie (1863) reported peat, twigs and branches in bedded sands and laminated clays beneath more than 30 m of till. In lowland Ayrshire in the Kilmaurs area (near Kilmarnock) organic remains occur in stratified deposits up to 11 m thick that are covered by till up to 23 m thick. The fossils obtained at various times since about the year 1816 include 9 or 10 mammoth tusks, a mammoth tooth, reindeer antlers, beetles, marine organisms and plant remains. The marine organisms include molluscs, foraminifers and ostracods indicative of arctic or subarctic conditions.

This evidence from Ayrshire and the Clyde basin, pointing to an advance of ice preceded by an interstadial (rather than an interglacial) was considered to relate to the Perth Readvance and an interstadial supposed to have occurred before it. This inter-pretation was in accord with a radiocarbon date of 13,700 (+1300, -1700) B.P. for a mammoth tusk from the Kilmaurs deposits (Sissons 1967b). The idea of the Perth Readvance was supported by McLellan (1969), who proposed modifications of the supposed limit in central Lanarkshire. However, the date of 27,550 (+1370, -1680) B.P. for the Bishopbriggs woolly rhino-ceros bone (p. 84) suggests that the evidence for ice advance relates to the build-up of the last ice-sheet following the inter-stadial that ended around 25,000 radiocarbon years ago. The date on the Kilmaurs mammoth tusk is made suspect by a radiocarbon date of greater than 40,000 B.P. obtained for a reindeer antler from the stratified deposits (Shotton *et al.* 1970). Furthermore, a date of greater than 36,900 B.P. for marine shells from fluvio-glacial deposits at Stranraer, just within the supposed limit of the Perth Readvance, does not accord with this supposed readvance. It must therefore be concluded that there is at present no firm evidence for a Perth Readvance or for other major readvances supposed to have interrupted the decay of the last ice-sheet.

Final decay of the ice-sheet
Fluvioglacial forms that occur in many parts of Scotland demonstrate widespread downwastage of the last ice-sheet (chapter 4). They show that, as downwasting proceeded moun-tains and hills gradually appeared above the ice surface, the ice becoming increasingly restricted to valley floors and basins. A

consequence was that often the ice became increasingly cut off from external sources of nourishment and hence its motion became more and more sluggish until, finally, in many areas it became stagnant or dead. Sugden (1970) argued that in the western Cairngorms and adjacent parts of Strathspey the ice-sheet survived throughout lateglacial times, finally decaying in the early postglacial (i.e. after *ca.* 10,300 B.P.). He considered the Loch Lomond Readvance to be represented by only a minor fluctuation of the margin of the ice-sheet. Peacock (1970) argued that the large volume of ice involved in the Loch Lomond Readvance in western Inverness-shire could not have accumulated in the time available and suggested that active ice existed in the area throughout lateglacial times. Yet the glaciers that built up during the readvance were not related to the remains of an ice-sheet for they were nourished on high ground, from which they often descended with steep gradients.

That most of Scotland was ice-free before the Loch Lomond Readvance occurred is proved by the 58 lateglacial pollen sites shown in figure 6.2, for at each of these sites the deposits of the Lateglacial Interstadial (i.e. the interstadial that preceded the Loch Lomond Readvance) have been recorded. Radiocarbon dates are available for several of the sites. The basal organic deposits at a site in Abernethy Forest, only a short distance from the western Cairngorms, gave a date of 12,710±270 B.P. (Y. Vasari, unpublished). At Loch Etteridge, located in upper Strathspey, the basal organic deposits were dated as 13,151±390 (Sissons and M.J.C. Walker 1974). Deposits from Loch Droma in the heart of the northwest Highlands provided a date of 12,810±155 (Kirk and Godwin 1963), while in the same area a date of 12,938±240 has been obtained for Cam Loch (W. Tutin, unpublished). The basal organic deposits from a kettle hole near Callander, located only 45 km from the centre of the greatest ice accumulation area in the British Isles, yielded a date of 12,750±120 (J.J. Lowe, unpublished) while similar deposits from a site near Drymen were dated as 12,510±310 (Y. Vasari, unpublished). A date of 12,940±250 B.P. relates to wood from a site near Lockerbie located 60 km from the major centre of ice accumulation in the Southern Uplands (Bishop 1963). In addition, the oldest dates for shells

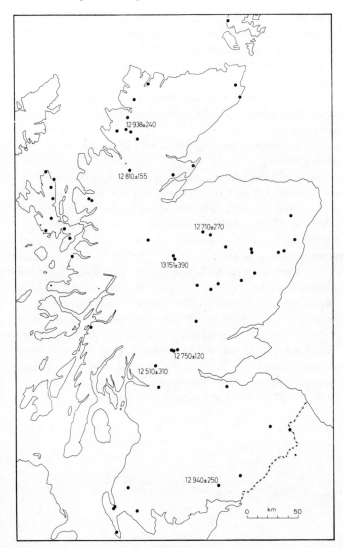

Fig. 6.2   Lateglacial pollen sites in Scotland and the oldest radiocarbon dates obtained for some of these sites. Based on published sources and on unpublished information provided by H.J.B. Birks, C.M. Clapperton, J.H. Dickson, S.E. Durno, R. Gunson, M. Jackes, J.J. Lowe, J. Macpherson, P.E. O'Sullivan, W. Tutin, M.J.C. Walker and Y. Vasari.

from marine deposits near Glasgow are 12,650±200, 12,610±210 and 12,615±230 B.P. (Bishop and Dickson 1970; Peacock 1971).

These dates, if valid, are minimal for ice-sheet decay. It is possible that some of them are too old owing to the 'hard water effect'. On the other hand, some of them relate to kettle holes where dead ice could have survived long after deglaciation of the surrounding ground. The dates therefore indicate that the ice-sheet had disappeared from a very large part of Scotland by 13,000 radiocarbon years ago or shortly after (Sissons and M.J.C. Walker 1974).

At around this time conditions appear to have become very unfavourable for ice-sheet survival. From the detailed study of beetle remains at a site in North Wales, Coope and Brophy (1972) concluded that rapid climatic amelioration occurred about 13,000 years ago with summer temperatures becoming at least as warm as those of the present day. The beetles from the radio-carbon-dated site near Lockerbie indicate July temperatures only marginally cooler than those of today (Coope, unpublished). It also appears that around 13,500 years ago polar water in the western Atlantic adjacent to the British Isles was replaced by warmer water, the polar water having retreated far to the west by 13,000 B.P. (Ruddiman and McIntyre 1973). It therefore seems unlikely that such remnants of the ice-sheet as survived at this time could have lasted much longer and total deglaciation by 12,500 radiocarbon years ago seems a conservative suggestion.

7 The Loch Lomond Readvance

It was the clear evidence for what is now termed the Loch Lomond Readvance that convinced the early glacialists in the 1840s that glaciers had once existed in Scotland. By the 1860s it was recognised that, following ice-sheet decay, there was a period of local glaciation in many Scottish uplands. This simple pattern subsequently became obscured by more elaborate, often conflicting, interpretations (chapter 6) and has emerged again only quite recently.

The limit of the readvance (fig. 7.1) is marked in many places by clear end moraines, over a hundred having been mapped. Outside the limit of the readvance such features are not known in Scotland. Ice decay following the readvance in many places left a highly-irregular morainic topography, sometimes comprising hundreds, or even thousands, of individual mounds scattered with great quantities of angular boulders. In some localities this morainic debris is arranged as fluted moraines, comprising straight or, more often, gently-curving ridges, varying from barely-distinguishable features to mounds 8 m high, that accurately record the latest directions of ice movement.

Radiocarbon dates and pollen sites

Radiocarbon dates directly related to the readvance are available from four sites, all of them being for marine shells. Ice-transported shells from the Menteith moraine at the head of the Forth lowlands gave a date of 11,800±170 B.P., shells from fluvioglacial deposits inside the Loch Lomond moraine were dated as 11,700±170, and shells from the Kinlochspelve moraine in eastern Mull provided a date of 11,330±170. Shells from glacially-disturbed marine clay beneath readvance deposits by Loch

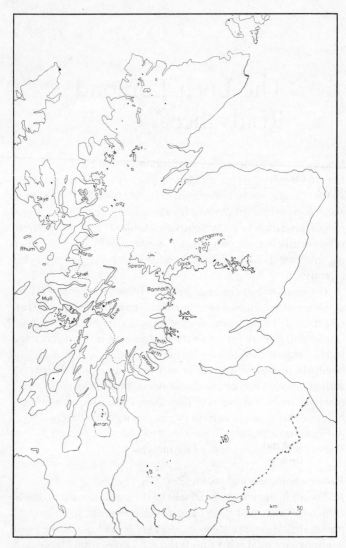

Fig. 7.1   Limit of the Loch Lomond Readvance. The limit has not yet been identified where a broken line is used. Based on published sources and on unpublished mapping by the author, along with information supplied by C.M. Clapperton, R. Cornish, M. Jackes, D. Rae, D.G. Sutherland and K.S.R. Thompson.

Creran, north of Oban, yielded dates of 11,430±220, 11,530±210 and 11,805±180 B.P. (Sissons 1967b; Peacock 1971; Gray and Brooks 1972). Since the only period after these dates cold enough to have permitted glaciers to develop occurred at the very end of the late-Devensian (between about 10,800 and about 10,300 B.P. or slightly later (but see p.106)), the readvance is assigned to this cold period.

The lateglacial pollen sites shown in figure 6.2 are very significant in relation to the Loch Lomond Readvance. In most sites a distinctive stratigraphy is present beneath the postglacial deposits. This comprises a basal minerogenic layer, followed by an organic layer relating to the Lateglacial Interstadial (or to part of it), succeeded by a minerogenic layer accumulated during the Loch Lomond Readvance (and, in some sites, also deposited partly during subsequent deglaciation). The lateglacial age of these deposits has been confirmed by radiocarbon dating at a considerable number of sites in Scotland. All the lateglacial pollen sites lie outside the limit of the Loch Lomond Readvance as determined from morphological evidence, some being located only one or two kilometres outside. They prove that the readvance failed to reach them. Lake deposits and peat inside the readvance limit have been shown by pollen analysis to relate only to postglacial times. Such sites have been investigated in the western Southern Uplands, the Forth and Teith valleys, Skye, and at several points in the Highlands (Donner 1957; Moar 1969; H.J.B. Birks, R. Gunson, J.J. Lowe and M.J.C. Walker, unpublished).

Glaciers of the Loch Lomond Readvance

The largest single ice mass that built up during the Loch Lomond Readvance was located in the western Grampians and in the mountainous ground west of the Great Glen. On the borders of the Grampians the ice spread out as piedmont lobes into the western Forth lowland and at the southern end of Loch Lomond. The Menteith end-moraine complex in the Forth valley extends for 20 km, varying from a single low ridge to a belt of features some hundreds of metres broad and up to 30 m high. It includes angular debris, large fluvioglacial accumulations and, in the lowest ground, much ice-transported marine clay with shells. The Loch

Lomond end-moraine complex varies similarly in composition and has been followed intermittently over a distance of 40 km, ranging in altitude from near sea-level to 300 m (J.B. Simpson 1933). The gradient of the moraine implies that over the deep rock basin of Loch Lomond some 25 to 30 km back from the ice limit the glacier was locally as much as 600 m thick. Towards the limit the crag-and-tail of Duncryne and a few drumlins record radial spreading in the piedmont terminal zone. The ice dammed up a lake in Strathblane and in the Endrick valley, proved by bottom deposits of silt and clay at least 12 m thick in the former. Accumulations of sand up to 30 m thick that were partly laid down amidst the ice during its subsequent decay were controlled by an englacial water-table, a prolongation of the lake level that was itself controlled by a col meltwater channel leading to the Forth valley.

In the Teith valley the ice limit is marked by an end moraine near Callander. Kettled kame terraces occur inside the moraine; outside it kettle-free outwash terraces extend intermittently down valley for 12 km, whereafter they are continued beneath the post-glacial raised mud flats of the Forth valley by a gravel fan with an area of at least 18 km^2 (Smith *et al.,* in the press). Farther north large glaciers, all part of the major ice mass in the southwest Grampians, terminated near the head of Loch Earn, reached the head of Loch Tay (Dochart and Lochay glaciers), occupied much of Glen Lyon, and extended to the eastern end of Loch Rannoch (K.S.R. Thompson 1972). In Glen Dochart fluvioglacial and morainic mounds, especially abundant on the floor of the glen and on its southern slope, show that the glacier surface rose quickly westwards, the ice being at least 270 m thick in its central part 5 km back from the terminus. The ice filled the Loch Rannoch trough and covered the broad bench that overlooks it to attain a maximal width of 12 km. Lateral moraines accurately define both margins of the glacier for many kilometres and extend intermittently for a total distance of 30 km. The outermost moraine is often very prominent and locally forms a rampart up to 30 m high across small side valleys. The ice margin sloped down eastwards at an average rate of 26 m/km for 10 km, there-after declining at 55 m/km for 3 km to its terminus beyond which, at the eastern end of Loch Rannoch, an outwash plain fills the valley floor.

The Rannoch glacier merged into a great accumulation of ice in the Rannoch basin that probably had an average depth of about 400 m over the lower ground. From this ice mass a glacier flowed north-eastwards to terminate part way along Loch Ericht, while another occupied Strath Ossian, where two end moraines, one within the other, mark two positions of its snout (fig. 7.2). Outwash from this glacier is seen as a delta measuring 1½ km in length and breadth that was built out into the Spean ice-dammed lake. This and the Roy and Gloy lakes were held up by ice from the Ben Nevis range (some of which flowed directly down the northern valleys of the range and some of which came through the Loch Treig glacial breach) and by ice from west of the Great Glen (fig. 4.3). The outermost end moraine in the Spean valley,

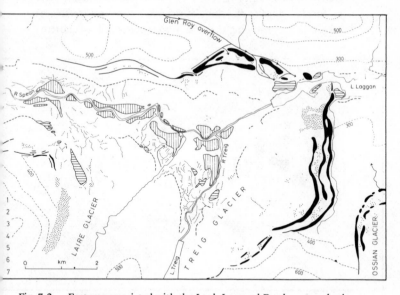

Fig. 7.2   Features associated with the Loch Lomond Readvance and sub-sequent deglaciation in the Spean-Treig area. 1. End moraines. 2. 'Parallel road' at 260 m. 3. Terraces related to 'parallel road'. 4. Later terraces. 5. Hummocky moraines. 6. Kames. 7. Meltwater channels. Kettle holes not shown.

first recognised by Jamieson (1863), is almost continuous for
15 km and locally forms a rampart over 10 m high (fig. 7.2). For
a short stretch a second end moraine parallels it while a third end
moraine extends for a considerable distance. Especially where all
three moraines are present boulders of Rannoch granite, many of
them 2 to 3 m long, occur in great numbers. In Glen Roy a
massive accumulation of drift occupies the floor of the southern
part of the glen and extends far up its sides. This drift mass has a
clear termination that declines steeply in altitude northwards on
both sides of the glen and defines the limit of the ice tongue that
dammed up the highest lake (cf. p. 71).

The limit of the major west Highland ice mass is not yet established in much of Argyllshire and western Inverness-shire, current
evidence relating mainly to a few valleys along the west coast. The
large outwash spreads at Corran by Loch Linnhe and at the
entrance to Loch Etive (p. 66) are generally considered to have
been formed close to the limit of the Loch Lomond Readvance,
the deep kettles showing that the outwash was at least partly

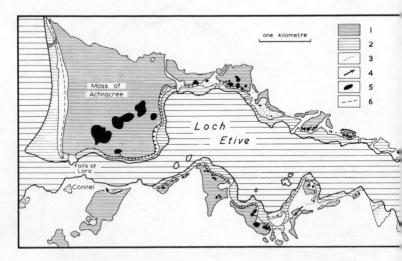

Fig. 7.3   Fluvioglacial landforms and raised marine features by Loch
Etive (after Gray 1972). 1. Kame terraces and outwash spreads. 2. Postglacial raised beaches. 3. Kames. 4. Meltwater channels. 5. Kettle holes.
6. Raised shingle ridges.

deposited on the respective ice tongues (fig. 7.3). Less impressive outwash spreads considered to have been formed at or close to the readvance limit occur at the western ends of lochs Morar and Shiel and at the entrance to Loch Creran. At Ballachullish, near the mouth of Loch Leven, extensive gravel deposits owe their present form to planation by the sea operating above its present level, but appear to have been deposited originally as outwash at or near the readvance limit (McCann 1966a; Peacock 1970; Gray 1972).

In northwest Scotland text-book examples of end moraines occur in dozens of places, defining precisely the limits of numerous former glaciers (although some glaciers did not produce such features). Some end moraines, such as the 30 m high Loch Gharbhrain moraine recording the former terminus of a valley glacier that was 10 km long, constitute prominent barriers across valley floors. Some record the arcuate limits of glaciers that flowed down tributary valleys to spread out on the floors of major valleys, as in Strath Dionard and at the head of Loch Torridon. One such glacier just managed to block the valley containing Loch na Sealga (fig. 7.4) to cause massive deposition of river gravels, kame terraces showing that the penned-up waters escaped between the glacier margin and the valley side against which it abutted. Some glaciers nourished in corries terminated part way down the sides of glacial troughs: normally their lateral moraines run steeply down the trough side and the frontal moraine is highly asymmetrical. Examples occur on the eastern side of An Teallach, high on the northern side of Glen Torridon and by Loch na Sealga (where one frontal moraine is up to 40 m high on its outer side and no more than 8 m on its inner side) (fig. 7.4).

Some glaciers in northwest Scotland terminated at the lip of the corrie that nourished them (e.g. Cul Mor) but others occupied only part of a corrie, sometimes being tiny features nestling under the part of the corrie wall most sheltered from direct insolation. In some corries moraines are absent, suggesting that glaciers failed to develop in them during the Loch Lomond Readvance (e.g. Ben Stack). On the other hand, end moraines show that in places small glaciers developed under sheltered rock walls at quite low altitudes. Two such glaciers existed at an altitude of 200 to 300 m on a rock bench beneath a northeast-facing rock wall by Little Loch Broom, while the end moraine of a similarly-located glacier near Gobernuisgach Lodge (south of Loch Hope) is at only 150-200 m.

While large boulders are common in many parts of the Highlands affected by the Loch Lomond Readvance, they occur in enormous quantities in parts of the northwest. This is especially true of the Torridon sandstone country, for this rock disintegrates into blocks typically 1-5 m long. Many end moraines and hummocky moraines are littered with such blocks, among which are occasional masses with volumes of hundreds of cubic metres, while some end moraines are entirely composed of piles of

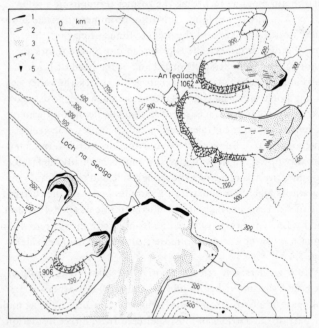

Fig. 7.4   Limit of the Loch Lomond Readvance around Loch na Sealga and An Teallach, northwest Scotland. 1. End moraines (and associated clear drift limits). 2. Fluted moraines. 3. Hummocky moraines (and, locally, fluvioglacial forms). 4. Inferred glacier limits. 5. Fossil frost wedge. Contour interval 100 m.

boulders with no visible fines. Among the most accessible
examples are the lateral moraines that define successive margins
of two glaciers that descended steeply to Loch Kishorn, the
former extent of the glacier termini being evident at low tide
from the distribution of boulders on the foreshore. In some
instances glacier limits are defined, not by end moraines, but by
an abrupt down-valley limit to abundant boulders (e.g.
Cranstackie). In other instances, however, this situation is
reversed: on steep valley sides boulders supplied by frost riving
may cover the ground above the former lateral margin of the
glacier but below it have been swept away by the glacier (e.g.
above the western margin of the large glacier that terminated by
Loch na Sealga).

Some of the glaciers in the northwest built a single end
moraine, such as the major feature holding back Loch Gharbhrain.
Sometimes there are two end moraines, one inside the other, as
over a total distance of 5 km on the valley slopes flanking
moraine-dammed Loch Ailsh. Three or four end moraines situated
close together mark successive positions of some glacier termini,
examples occurring by Loch Kishorn, by Loch na Sealga (fig. 7.4)
and by the eastern end of Loch Fannich.

Excellent examples of fluted moraines are common in the
northwest, those in Strath Dionard being particularly noteworthy
in that they are superimposed on large mounds and dead-ice
hollows, implying that active ice over-rode dead ice. Another
interesting feature is an example of a formerly ice-cored end
moraine north of Ben More Assynt, demonstrated by deep kettles
that cause a steep-sided, boulder-strewn moraine ridge to split
temporarily into two lesser ridges. In the same area former ice
cores are recorded by mounds with a central depression. The
northwest also has the finest examples of hummocky moraines in
the British Isles, with the Valley of the Hundred Hills by Glen
Torridon the most easily reached, although much more massive
and extensive features exist a short distance to the north in the
Beinn Eighe Nature Reserve.

In the central Grampians an ice-cap with an area of nearly
300 km^2 and a volume of about 32 km^3 was nourished on the
Gaick plateau, situated between Glen Tilt and the Pass of

Drumochter (Sissons 1974a). From it small outlet glaciers radiated down numerous valleys, some of them descending steeply to adjacent lower ground. Outwash terraces often begin at or within the former limits of these outlet glaciers, while in many valleys hummocky moraines abound, the most accessible example of these forms being the excellent features that extend for 14 km on both sides of the A9 road from upper Glen Garry through the Pass of Drumochter into Glen Truim. In these two glens and some others the abrupt down-valley termination of hummocky moraines marks the former ice limit. Especially on the higher ground, systems of very small meltwater channels characterise many areas covered by the ice-cap (fig. 4.2). On the other hand, end moraines are very rare and where they do occur are poorly developed. Although extensive, the average thickness of the ice-cap and associated outlet glaciers was only 110 m, its greatest thickness being about 380 m.

Farther east in the Grampians on the plateau between glens Clova, Muick and Esk an ice-cap with an area of about 65 km^2 built up during the Loch Lomond Readvance (fig. 7.5). End moraines are absent, the limits of the three principal outlet glaciers being marked by the sharp down-valley termination of hummocky moraines at or within which low outwash terraces begin (Sissons 1972a). Elsewhere in the eastern half of the Grampians there were considerable valley glaciers, corrie glaciers, and small glaciers that developed in sheltered valley heads (fig. 7.5). The larger glaciers, such as those that existed in glens Clova, Callater and Muick, were up to 10 km in length and locally exceeded 200 m in depth, although their average depth was less than 100 m. Glaciers descended steeply into some glens from accumulation areas in rather shallow plateau valleys: thus the surface of the glacier that flowed down into the Glen Clova trough declined 600 m in 5 km, while the comparable figures for the adjacent Glen Doll glacier are 450 m and 3 km. End moraines, normally composed largely or entirely of boulders, were frequently formed by corrie and valley-head glaciers in the eastern Grampians. Normally 1 to 10 m high and up to 2 km long, they are known from the eastern Cairngorms (C.M. Clapperton, unpublished), western Cairngorms, Lochnagar, Mount Keen and the

Glen Esk and Glen Clova areas (Sissons and Grant 1972).

Much farther south, just over the Border, glacier ice accumulated on a very small scale in the shelter of The Cheviot (Clapperton 1970). In the centre of the Southern Uplands in the Tweedsmuir Hills the former existence of glaciers up to a few kilometres long is indicated particularly by hummocky moraines, which are especially numerous near the Loch Skene corrie. In the hills that surround the Loch Doon basin high ground is less extensive and small glaciers developed in a few sheltered locations, their limits at The Tauchers and Loch Dungeon being recorded by clear end moraines.

The limit of the readvance in Arran was mapped by Gemmell (1973) but it seems more likely that only the fresh, steep-sided

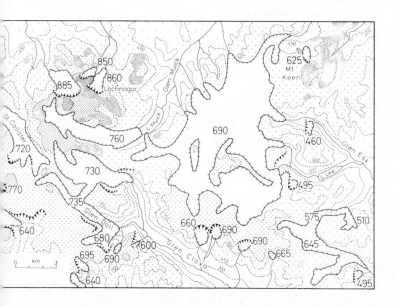

Fig. 7.5   Limit of the Loch Lomond Readvance in the southeast Grampians, based on Sissons (1972a) and Sissons and Grant (1972). Contour interval 150 m. Values attached to glaciers are firn lines (metres) calculated for the time the glaciers were at their maximal extent. Oblique shading locates areas where fossil periglacial forms (especially boulder lobes) are common.

moraines studded with boulders that he described as occurring mainly in corries on the eastern flanks of the Goatfell ridge are related to the readvance. Gray and Brooks (1972) mapped the former limits of an ice-cap and small independent glaciers in eastern Mull, where hummocky and fluted moraines are widespread. Nunataks rose above the surface of the ice-cap and outlet glaciers descended to sea-level along Glen Forsa, at the heads of Loch na Keal and Loch Buie, and in lochs Don and Spelve. The two last-named sea lochs were occupied by a piedmont glacier whose limit is partly defined by end-moraine ridges that locally contain ice-transported marine shells. End moraines frequently record the readvance limit in Skye. Figure 7.6 shows the extent of five small glaciers that accumulated in corries on the west and south-west flanks of the Cuillins, each terminus being defined by an arcuate boulder moraine. In Orkney only one tiny glacier formed during the Loch Lomond Readvance, its limit marked by the well-defined Enegars moraine in northern Hoy (D. Rae, unpublished).

Climatic considerations
The preceding account of glaciers that built up during the Loch Lomond Readvance is incomplete, partly because space does not permit reference to many of the glaciers that existed at the time, and partly because detailed evidence is not yet available for considerable areas. When this evidence is complete detailed palaeoclimatic reconstructions will be possible. At present certain limited inferences can be made.

That precipitation was high in the western Grampians and southern part of the northern Highlands is evident from the much greater extent and thickness of the glaciers compared with those in the east. In accord with this, fluvioglacial deposits associated with the readvance and subsequent deglaciation are far more massive in the west (e.g. by Loch Etive, at Corran by Loch Linnhe, and in Glen Spean and the adjacent part of the Great Glen), although their areas of occurrence are restricted owing to steep valley sides and because meltwaters could often escape freely down valley. The high western precipitation was the major factor in the westward decrease in firn line altitude, evident from the much lower altitudes at which glaciers were able to accumulate and to which they descended in the west.

Since the evidence for the former glaciers is often plentiful and strict constraints on their dimensions are usually imposed by the

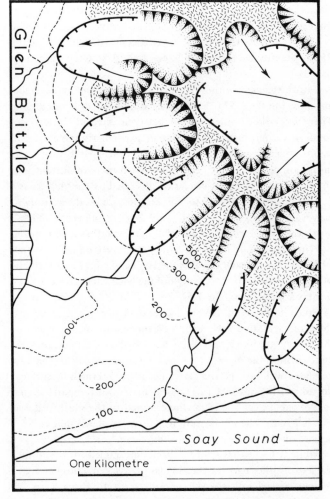

Fig. 7.6   Limits of corrie glaciers of the Loch Lomond Readvance in part of the Cuillin Hills, Skye.

marked relief, approximate contours for the surfaces of the glaciers when at their greatest extent can be drawn. On the reasonable approximation that ablation and accumulation were linearly related to altitude, the firn line for the time a glacier was in equilibrium at its maximal extent can be simply calculated from the areas between successive contours. For the Gaick plateau ice-cap in the central Grampians the calculated firn line is 790 m (Sissons 1974a), a value that contrasts with the figure of 250 m determined for the Mull ice-cap by J.M. Gray (unpublished).

For the glaciers in the southeast Grampians (many of which are shown in fig. 7.5) firn lines ranged between 460 and 880 m. There was considerable variation between adjacent glaciers, a result of various factors, aspect being particularly important. Its significance lay only to a slight extent in the shelter from direct insolation provided by steep slopes: much more important was the proportion of direct insolation absorbed by the glaciers as determined by their angle to the sun. Despite local variations, however, the firn line rose markedly towards the north and northwest, suggesting that snowfall in the southeast Grampians was brought mainly by winds from a southerly point. Snowfall must have been heavy towards the Highland edge (as it is today with such winds) for here, overlooking Glen Clova, south-facing glaciers accumulated (fig. 7.5).

Precipitation contrasts are also evident in relation to part of the Gaick ice-cap. In the northwest the major outlet glacier of the ice-cap, despite a strong northerly surface gradient, terminated within the plateau area, but in the southwest the ice-cap extended well beyond the plateau edge even though its surface sloped southwards. The firn line calculated for the northwestern part of the ice-cap is 815 m whereas that for the southwestern part is 740 m. The implication is that snowfall was much heavier on the southern side of the ice-cap.

While firn lines have not yet been determined for the former glaciers of other parts of the Highlands, marked contrasts are evident in glacier distribution in quite short distances. Thus while major glaciers from the Rannoch ice reservoir extended to Loch Laggan and its vicinity, the mountains on either side of the loch, with numerous summits exceeding 1000 m and a series of corries, possessed only one glacier exceeding a kilometre in length (fig. 4.3). On the coast of Wester Ross glaciers descended to sea-level at lochs Carron, Kishorn and Torridon and a small glacier was able to develop at an altitude of only 200 m by Little Loch Broom. Yet in Easter Ross the Ben Wyvis range, which rises above 1000 m and includes steep, sheltered rock slopes, failed to nourish glaciers during the readvance.

The broad pattern of glacier distribution in the Highlands during the Loch Lomond Readvance thus indicates a firn line rising rapidly into the interior from the west coast and, in the east, from the border with the Central Lowlands. In part this reflects the well-known 'rain shadow' effect, which would be increasingly emphasised by the glaciers themselves as they built up. It also suggests, as noted above, that winds from the south brought the main snowfalls in the east: in the west, winds from south-west were probably most important in this respect. One may envisage that, favoured by lower temperatures, a more powerful winter anticyclone than now existed over the continent, its frequent extension across the site of the North Sea being encouraged by the southern part of that sea being a land area (world sea-level being lower) and the northern part probably being partly or wholly frozen in winter. Fronts approaching from the Atlantic would frequently be slowed down as they approached the high pressure area, resulting in the 'south-wind snowstorms' whose importance in glacial times was stressed by Manley (1952, 219-24).

From the glacier firn lines July temperatures at the time the ice was at its greatest extent may be inferred using data provided by Ahlmann (1948) for modern Norwegian glaciers. Assuming precipitation in the Gaick area was 80% of its present value, a July mean temperature of about $3°C$ at the 790 m firn line is indicated, corresponding to a sea-level temperature of about $7.5°C$. When the ice-cap was building up the firn line was lower, but is unlikely to have been much below 700 m since otherwise some areas that were ice-free could hardly have remained so. Thus a July temperature equivalent to $7°C$ at sea-level seems likely, a figure that may be compared with 7.5 to $8°C$ estimated by

Manley (1964) for Windermere and 10°C or just below proposed
by Coope *et al.* (1971) for the English Midlands.

While it is normally assumed that the Loch Lomond
Readvance began about 10,800 B.P., the combined evidence of
Manley and Coope *et al.* suggests otherwise. The latter (1971)
have inferred from Coleoptera obtained from sites in England,
Wales and the Isle of Man that a fall of temperature that began
over 12,000 radiocarbon years ago continued to the end of the
Lateglacial Interstadial, by which time mean July temperatures
were probably 4-5°C below present values. Since Manley (1949)
concluded that a fall in mean summer temperature of at least 2°C
from present values would cause glaciers to develop on Ben Nevis,
while Coope *et al.* considered the interstadial climate to be
moderately continental (implying that winter temperatures by the
end of the interstadial were more than 4-5°C below present), it
appears that the Loch Lomond Readvance began before, perhaps
well before, 10,800 B.P. The glaciers would begin to develop at
different times in different places, as influenced by such factors
as relief and precipitation. Radiocarbon dates from certain widely
scattered sites in Scotland and elsewhere in Britain show that
organic deposition in kettle holes and similar sites terminated
about 10,800 radiocarbon years ago, suggesting a final rather
abrupt climatic deterioration at this time.

The cold climate of the stadial is generally considered to have
lasted until about 10,300 B.P., suggesting that the glaciers
probably attained their greatest extent at this time. That many
glaciers remained at or close to their limit for some time is indicated by the abundance of end moraines. Sometimes there is a
major end moraine, sometimes a broad end moraine zone, in
some cases two distinct moraines occur, while a number of
glaciers produced three or four end moraines. Despite these
differences, however, these indicators of glacial equilibrium are
restricted to a zone no more than a few hundred metres broad at
the outer limit of the former glaciers. Inside this zone end
moraines are virtually absent, only two instances being currently
known to the author (in the Loch Skene corrie in the central
Southern Uplands and near Ben More Assynt in northwest Scotland). Since this pattern is widespread in the Highlands and

applies to valley glaciers, piedmont glaciers and corrie glaciers, it has climatic implications. It indicates that the main cold period of the stadial was succeeded by a slight amelioration of climate or, more probably by a slight amelioration interrupted by cold spells, to be followed in turn by a climatic improvement that caused general glacier decay, in some instances at least leading to widespread stagnation of the ice. It seems likely that the beginning of general glacier decay coincided approximately with the very rapid increase of summer temperatures (approaching 17°C for July) reported by Coope *et al.* from the English Midlands. How long the glaciers took to decay is not yet established, but it doubtless varied considerably depending on such factors as glacier size, aspect and altitude (Sissons 1974c).

8   Periglacial features

Periglacial features cover the higher parts of many Scottish mountains and comprise both fossil and active forms. There is also clear evidence that in the past periglacial processes operated down to sea-level over much of the country. Yet, despite widespread periglacial activity, the forms now visible represent only a minor modification of the land surface that has taken place during and since the decay of the last ice-sheet. Periglacial processes must have operated for lengthy periods during and before the build-up of the last ice-sheet but, apart from a few fossil frost wedges, the glaciers themselves appear to have removed or obliterated the evidence. Hence Scotland does not have thick accumulations of soliflucted material such as occur at the foot of slopes in southern England beyond the limits of the successive ice-sheets.

Active features

Minor periglacial features, such as small stone polygons and stone stripes, ploughing boulders, solifluction terraces and some solifluction lobes are active today. This is hardly surprising in view of the harsh winters that prevail on the Scottish mountains: gales are frequent, precipitation is heavy, and on the highest ground mean temperatures for several months may be below freezing point but with frequent rises of temperature above zero. The records of the observatory maintained on the summit of Ben Nevis from 1884 to 1896 indicate a mean annual temperature there of $-0.4°$C, the February mean being $-4.6°$C.

That stone stripes on Tinto Hill in Lanarkshire are currently active was effectively shown by Miller *et al.* (1954) for, having destroyed a small area of stripes, it was found that the stripes had re-formed two years later when the site was revisited. Ryder and

McCann (1971) argued that stone stripes in Rhum are active because they have not been destroyed by treading by the many deer in the area. Having disturbed polygons in the Cairngorms, King (1971a) attempted to measure subsequent movement of the constituent materials. In some instances clear evidence of movement of stones and soil was obtained although there was no sign that the polygons were re-forming.

Solifluction terraces with vegetated fronts typically half to one metre high and almost unvegetated treads one to ten metres broad appear to be most common in very exposed locations such as spur crests and mountain ridges. The spilling of debris from the treads onto the vegetated risers points to current activity. The down-slope movement of individual boulders in many areas of high ground in Scotland is indicated by bow waves of debris and vegetation pushed up in front of them, the tracks they have followed being marked by depressions typically 1-3 m long but occasionally much longer. Present movement of such ploughing boulders has been demonstrated by measurements by R. Shaw (unpublished).

King (1971b) stated that much of the ground above 450 m in the Cairngorms has been denuded of vegetation to form bare patches that are usually about a metre wide and 2 to 4 m long, although very occasionally much larger. He concluded that these 'denuded surfaces' are caused by the action of needle ice and by deflation, although the treading of deer and man are significant in some instances. As King pointed out, similar denuded surfaces are widespread in the Highlands. Wind action is especially significant on some of the Torridon sandstone mountains of northwest Scotland (e.g. Quinag and particularly An Teallach) for here large areas, including many steep slopes, are covered with sheets of sand up to several metres thick. The surfaces of the sand sheets are normally well vegetated, but in places they are cut off abruptly by steep bare slopes that border areas of poorly-vegetated stony ground up to hundreds of metres across from which the sand has been removed mainly by wind. It is not known when the sand sheets accumulated or when their dissection began.

The lower limit of present-day periglacial activity is very variable but over much of the Scottish mainland it appears to be in the range 450 to 600 m. However, in the north the level down to which periglacial processes operate descends markedly. On the granite of Ronas Hill in Mainland Shetland well-developed active solifluction terraces cover an extensive area above about 300 m altitude, while on the island of Unst small stone stripes are active at an altitude of only 60 m (Ball and Goodier 1974).

Fossil features

Although periglacial processes operate today on the Scottish mountains it is generally agreed that they were more effective in times past. Radiocarbon dates of 4880±135 and 2680±120 B.P. have been obtained for organic material buried by solifluction lobes in the Cairngorms and a date of 5145±135 B.P. was provided by similar material found beneath a solifluction terrace on Arkle in northwest Scotland. Sugden (1971) and White and Mottershead (1972) suggested around 500 B.C. and the sixteenth to eighteenth centuries as the most probable times for this solifluction to have taken place. King (1971a) tentatively inferred from lichen measurements that coarse polygons and stripes he investigated in the Cairngorms were produced in the eighteenth and nineteenth centuries.

This postglacial activity is minor, however, compared with that of lateglacial times. Some of the fossil periglacial features on the Scottish mountains may have been formed when the lower ground was still covered by the downwasting ice-sheet, but the severe climatic conditions that accompanied the Loch Lomond Readvance were of major importance. The periglacial landscape of the mountains is essentially a fossil landscape that has been modified only in detail, although often intricately, since the end of glacial times.

Evidence of former severe climatic conditions is provided by fossil frost wedges. A few wedges near Glasgow and Edinburgh occur in fluvioglacial deposits overlain by glacial till, indicating that they were formed before the last ice-sheet finally covered the respective areas. Fossil wedges at more than 70 other sites in Scotland extend down from the present ground surface or, more commonly, begin a little below the surface. Most of them extend down 1½ to 3 m, but some attain 4 to 5 m. One has been found in shale bedrock (McManus 1966). The vast majority have been discovered in sections in kames, outwash spreads and raised beaches and must therefore have developed since glacier ice last covered the sites at which they occur. Since many of the wedges are on low ground and since they have been found on the west side of the country as well as in the east (where finds are most numerous), it is clear that permanently frozen ground existed in Scotland down to sea-level during and/or after the decay of the last ice-sheet (Sissons 1974c).

Fossil frost wedges at a site in northwest Scotland (fig. 7.4) and at two sites in Mull are located on low ground just inside the limit of the Loch Lomond Readvance (J.S. Bibby, unpublished; Sissons, unpublished). The evidence from pollen sites in Scotland excludes the possibility that these wedges were formed after the last glaciers had wasted away. Hence it appears they developed during the period when the glaciers withdrew slightly from their maximal limits (p. 107). Péwé (1966) concluded that a mean annual temperature at least as low as $-6°C$ is necessary for frost wedges to develop in Alaska. Since J.M. Gray's unpublished data for the firn line in Mull when the glaciers of the Loch Lomond Readvance were at their maximal extent imply a mean July temperature at sea-level of $5°C$, it may seem that the mean January sea-level temperature at this time in western Scotland was at least $-17°C$. However, since many factors affect the development of frost wedges and more data are needed from areas where wedges are forming today, this figure must be regarded as very tentative. A January mean temperature of at least $-7°C$ is implied since a mean annual temperature no higher than about $-1°C$ is required for permafrost to develop (other than in peat bogs).

Solifluction sheets are widespread on many areas of high ground with gentle to moderate slopes. They often terminate abruptly part way down the mountain side in a sharp descent half a metre to several metres high. Springs issue from the base of this riser, the drainage of the solifluction sheets normally being below the surface owing to their coarse composition. Such material is widespread in the Southern Uplands above about

450 m and was investigated in detail by Ragg and Bibby (1966) on Broad Law, where the stony stratified deposits were found to be up to 3.5 m thick. That these deposits ceased to accumulate when climate ameliorated following the Loch Lomond Readvance is suggested by their apparent absence from ground covered by the glaciers involved in the readvance as, for example, in and near the Loch Skene corrie situated only a few kilometres from Broad Law. Meltwater channels are also significant in this context. On the Gaick plateau in the central Grampians clear meltwater channels as little as a metre deep and two metres wide run along slopes up to altitudes exceeding 800 m on ground covered by an ice-cap during the Loch Lomond Readvance (fig. 4.2). Since such small channels are highly susceptible to obliteration by debris moving down slope their survival means that little or no solifluction has occurred here since the ice-cap decayed. In contrast, bigger meltwater channels at 800-900 m altitude on the mountains north of Loch Laggan in ground not covered by glaciers during the readvance are largely infilled with coarse debris produced by frost-shattering of their sides.

Solifluction at an altitude of only 150 m or so during the stadial is indicated by series of radiocarbon dates for organic layers related to solifluction deposits near Keith in Banffshire and near Langholm in Dumfriesshire, while its common occurrence on low ground at this time is implied by minerogenic sediments in numerous lateglacial pollen sites, the pollen and related studies pointing to an incomplete plant cover (e.g. Pennington *et al.* 1972). No distinct forms have yet been reported as associated with this low-altitude solifluction.

Solifluction sheets on the mountains may terminate down slope in series of lobes, each lobe typically some 10 to 30 m across. Often the crenulate edges of successive sheets appear one above the other on a mountain side. In other instances the solifluction lobes occur in small groups or, occasionally, in isolation. Lobes are most conspicuous when composed of boulders, as in many granite areas. Here lobe fronts may rise 5 m or more and the boulders may average a metre in diameter. On Lochnagar and Mount Keen in the southeast Grampians such massive lobes abound down to altitudes varying between 700 and 500 m but are absent from ground covered by glaciers during the Loch Lomond Readvance (fig. 7.5). Even in corries at altitudes of 900 to 1000 m the lobes do not occur within the former ice limit, despite the abundance of boulders, and lateral boulder moraines can be followed across steeply-sloping ground (Sissons and Grant 1972).

The gentle slopes of many high interfluves and summits are extensively covered with frost-shattered rock debris so that firm bedrock is rarely seen. The debris is most obvious on rocks that disintegrate, at least in part, into large fragments, giving rise to blockfields, as on the granophyre of western Rhum (Ryder and McCann 1971), on the quartzite summit of Schiehallion in the central Grampians, and on the granite of the Cairngorms. Quartzite is particularly susceptible to frost action: in northwest Scotland, for example, the quartzite is associated with extensive scree slopes. On the western side of Arkle tongues of fresh almost-white quartzite debris on the upper parts of the screes are replaced at lower levels by debris of darker shades of grey, indicating that the massive screes are only partly active. The great screes on Rhum were investigated by Ryder and McCann, who concluded that, while postglacial scree formation has been significant, there appears to have been a major period of scree development at the very end of lateglacial times. In addition to the innumerable obvious bare scree slopes in the Highlands and Southern Uplands many steep regular slopes beneath rock faces are composed of angular debris now concealed by vegetation. Such screes are clearly fossil.

Certain rather shallow perched corrie-like features in the Red Hills in Skye were interpreted by Birks (1973) as nivation hollows. He suggested that during the Loch Lomond Stadial they were occupied by permanent snow beds at the edges of which protalus ramparts accumulated. Perhaps the best example of such a rampart in Scotland is situated at the foot of Baosbheinn 10 km south-south-east of Gairloch in Wester Ross. The rampart curves round the northern base of the mountain for a kilometre and is up to 8 m high on its inside and up to 55 m on its steep outer side. The ridge is composed of blocks of Torridon sandstone, many of which are 1-4 m long. That the blocks slid down a snow slope is indicated, not only by the depression between ridge crest and mountain foot, but also by the steep outward dip of a high proportion of the blocks. Yet at the present time snow does not accumulate here in significant amounts while the scree that rises for 200 m behind the rampart is vegetated except where scattered relatively-small blocks lie on it. Thus the feature is fossil and it was most probably formed during the Loch Lomond Stadial.

Evidence of former landslides is very common in the Scottish uplands, particularly in the Highlands and some of the islands. The most remarkable examples are in northern Skye (p. 19) but these are not typical of landslides in the Highlands and islands generally. The typical landslide is entirely in rigid rocks and has normally involved corrie walls or the sides of U-shaped troughs. Some landslides descended to valley floors, such as one that blocked a small valley by Glen Coe to produce a temporary lake now revealed by an alluvial flat (Bailey *et al.* 1916). More often the debris litters the valley side and consists of a chaos of blocks below a rock scar. In other cases a single mass of rock that may be hundreds of metres long has clearly slid down from its original position. Numerous landslides have involved only limited movements: thus along the walls of corries slices of rock have sometimes moved down a few tens of metres or may only have moved enough to leave a deep crack in the ground surface. Similar cracks sometimes occur on trough sides, occasionally attaining lengths of hundreds of metres.

That landslides have occurred in postglacial times is demonstrated by the record of one having taken place in Arran some 250 years ago, its size being sufficient to cause it to be heard tens of kilometres away. It seems likely, however, that the great majority of the slides were produced in lateglacial times. Direct evidence is lacking for, apart from the Skye landslides, which have probably had a long and complex history, landslides in Scotland have not been studied in detail. Yet, especially during the Loch Lomond Stadial, when permafrost existed down to sea-level, the formation of ice wedges along, for example, major joint planes, must have been a potent factor in their production.

A major landslide that descended from Beinn Alligin in Wester Ross appears to have had unusual consequences. Extending for

1.2 km from the base of the steep mountain slope is a sharply-defined tapering tongue of debris that rises to a maximal height of 12-15 m and consists of a mass of Torridon sandstone blocks up to 5 m or more long. The highly irregular surface of the mass comprises ridges and depressions, some of the former being well-marked transverse features with steep fronts that include many blocks dipping steeply down slope, giving the impression that the debris has been pushed along and has slipped down in front of a huge bulldozer. The distance the debris extends from the mountain foot down a relatively gentle slope, the lack of fine material, and the sharply-defined edges of the mass, appear inconsistent with an explanation of the feature by landsliding alone. Rather does it appear that the landslide debris descended onto a decaying remnant of glacier ice (following the Loch Lomond Readvance), temporarily reactivating it to produce a rock glacier now preserved in fossil form.

Tors occur on a number of mountains in Scotland and are associated with various types of rock. Those on the summits of Morven, Smean and Maiden Pap in Caithness are formed of conglomerate while on Ben Loyal in Sutherland they are composed of syenite. They are best developed in granite, however, with the Cairngorms, where they stand as much as 25 m high, providing the best and most numerous examples. Their distribution is related to glacial activity: good examples appear to be absent from the intensely-glaciated areas of western Scotland, while in the Cairngorms they are largest and most numerous in the north and northeast where they were most sheltered from the major ice-stream that came from the southwest. Thus tors in general must pre-date the last ice-sheet. Linton (1955) maintained that they are essentially a product of Tertiary weathering, their specific locations being related to more widely-spaced joints. They have presumably been modified by periglacial processes in lateglacial times and it is possible that some small ones developed entirely under periglacial conditions.

Specific studies of the action of non-glacial rivers during the Loch Lomond Stadial have not been attempted, although there are hints that it was important. That the large fans at the foot of the Ochil fault-line scarp east of Stirling date back in part to lateglacial times is demonstrated by their relation to raised beaches (Kemp 1971). In Glen Roy the accumulations of debris discharged into the former ice-dammed lake from glacier-free tributary valleys demonstrate the effectiveness of some rivers during the Loch Lomond Stadial. In Edinburgh the lake deposits that accumulated during the Lateglacial Interstadial at Corstorphine (Newey 1970) are extensively covered by a broad fan of sand and gravel laid down by the Water of Leith. Only postglacial lake deposits overlie the sand and gravel, implying that the fan was built up during the Loch Lomond Stadial. It is reasonable to infer that many other alluvial fans in Scotland were formed or largely built up at this time, their development being favoured by the absence of blanket peat, sparse vegetation, feeble soil development and frozen ground, all of which would encourage rapid run-off. It may also be surmised that the frozen ground in particular would encourage lateral movement of the larger streams and hence that the extent of many present-day floodplains was largely determined during this period.

Spreads of fluvioglacial sand are quite often dissected by small dry valleys that may well have been excavated when permafrost existed (e.g. in East Lothian). Similar valleys are common in lateglacial raised beach deposits in southeast Scotland, where some attain depths of 15-20 m and a width between their upper edges of 300 m. The lower parts of some of these valleys contain raised beach deposits that date back to at least 9600 B.P., showing that the valleys are of greater age. The buried floors of the valleys are broad and veneered with gravel, contrasting with their tiny present-day successors cut in postglacial deposits and containing only sand. The fossil valleys are most readily explained as formed during the harsh conditions of the Loch Lomond Stadial. They relate to a period of low sea-level when powerful marine erosion occurred, yet another consequence of the climatic conditions of the stadial (p. 123).

9 Relative changes of sea-level

The most obvious evidence of past changes in the relative levels of land and sea around the coasts of Scotland comprises raised beaches, raised rock platforms and raised cliffs, but some old marine forms lie below sea-level while others are buried beneath later deposits. Much the greater part of this evidence relates to changes that occurred during and after the decay of the last ice-sheet.

The two principal factors involved in the lateglacial and post-glacial land/sea-level movements were eustatic changes of sea-level, related particularly to changing volumes of the world's glaciers, and isostatic uplift of Scotland, related to removal of its own ice load. The general result of the latter factor, first appreciated by Jamieson as long ago as 1865, is that raised marine features increase in altitude towards the major centre of glacier accumulation in Scotland (Rannoch Moor and vicinity). In peripheral areas, such as Orkney and Shetland, there is evidence only of submergence, for here world sea-level rise has exceeded isostatic recovery.

Raised beaches extend along much of the coast of eastern and southwestern Scotland and are especially extensive in the more sheltered areas such as the inner Moray Firth, the firths of Forth and Tay, the Clyde estuary, the Ayrshire lowlands and the indentations of the Solway coast. In each of these areas they occupy tens of square kilometres and in the Forth valley the marine and estuarine deposits locally exceed 100 m in thickness. On the west coast of the Highlands and around the inner islands raised beaches are often much more fragmentary. On the other hand, in parts of the west there are striking raised marine features cut in solid rock.

Especially in more sheltered localities the lateglacial marine sediments consist of layers of sand, silt and clay that frequently contain ice-rafted stones. Ice rafting was neatly demonstrated by Jamieson's (1865) discovery in clay pits at Paisley of barnacles on the undersides of boulders. The lateglacial sediments are usually concealed by postglacial marine and estuarine deposits along the coast itself, but inland they often emerge to form series of raised beaches. Some of these beaches merge into outwash spreads, thus allowing former sea-levels to be linked with former positions of glacier margins. In exposed locations raised shingle ridges may occur, the most remarkable examples being in western Jura and northern Islay. These ridges, typically curved, range in altitude between about 14 and 38 m and together extend for kilometres. Composed of rounded quartzite cobbles, they are often conspicuous owing to lack of vegetation (McCann 1964). Another feature of the lateglacial marine deposits is that in eastern Scotland the great bulk of them is typified by an arctic fauna and shells are relatively scarce. In the west, however, especially in the Clyde area where shell beds abound, a subarctic fauna is characteristic.

In certain sheltered areas, especially by the Firth of Tay, in the Forth valley, by the Clyde estuary and along part of the Solway coast, postglacial estuarine sedimentation is represented by extensive raised mud flats known in Scotland as 'carse'. Much, but certainly not all of the carse was originally covered with peat up to 5 or 6 m thick. Extensive areas of peat have been removed by man but isolated islands remain and in the western Forth valley there are still some broad spreads (e.g. Flanders Moss). The postglacial raised beaches are composed of sand and shingle in less sheltered areas and often contain large quantities of shells. In some localities raised shingle ridges are common. Good examples exist northwards from Montrose (Crofts 1972) but the most elaborate systems are on the coasts of the Moray Firth, especially around Lossiemouth, and were mapped in detail by Olgilvie (1923).

Interglacial rock platforms and cliffs
A raised rock platform and cliff, with a shoreline varying in alti-

tude between about 25 and 45 m, has been described as occurring
in the Inner Hebrides from Skye and Raasay in the north to Jura
and Islay in the south, as well as occasionally on the adjacent
mainland coast (W.B. Wright 1911; McCann 1968; Ryder 1968;
Richards 1969; McCann and Richards 1969). The features are
best developed on west-facing coasts and on some of these are
locally very prominent, the platform rising gently landwards over
a distance as great as 800 m and the degraded cliff behind
occasionally exceeding 60 m in height. The considerable variations in altitude of the shoreline over the Inner Hebrides as a
whole are attributed to tectonic warping. The platform is said to
be striated and ice-moulded in places and in some localities glacial
till is said to lie on it. The rock features are therefore considered
to pre-date at least the last ice-sheet but a preglacial age is considered unlikely because of their extent and clarity in some areas.

In eastern Scotland rock platform remnants between altitudes
of about 18 and 25 m occur between North Berwick (in East
Lothian) and Berwick. A small rock hill rising above the extensive
platform remnant on which part of Dunbar is built forms the crag
of a crag-and-tail, the tail descending below the level of the platform to low ground on its inland side. The clear preservation of
the tail shows that it was formed later than the platform and
hence that the latter pre-dates the last ice-sheet.

Along the same stretch of the east coast a marine abrasion
platform up to several hundred metres broad that lies between
present tide-marks appears unlikely to have been formed recently
in view of the limited time the sea has been at its present level in
recent times. At various localities (e.g. near Dunbar) the platform
is terminated inland by a tiny rock cliff a metre or two high,
inland from which is a rock platform that passes beneath raised
beach deposits. It may well be that the two platforms were
originally one, the work of the sea in recent times having been
restricted to the cutting of the step that now separates them.

Farther north on the east coast, at St Andrews, borehole data
show that a low-level rock platform pre-dates the last ice-sheet,
for the platform (and the cliff that backs it) are covered by postglacial and lateglacial raised beach deposits, the latter merging
into glacial outwash (Cullingford 1972). In northeast Scotland

and Caithness some of the deep narrow gashes in the cliffs contain glacial till. In the former area a low-level rock platform partly exhumed from a cover of glacial drift has been described (Walton 1959), while on the opposite side of the country in Kintyre rock stacks encased in till have been reported. Collectively such features imply that many rock-cut marine features of the Scottish coastline pre-date at least the last glaciation and suggest that the sea in lateglacial and postglacial times has been mainly engaged in removing drift deposits of various types to reveal the ancient rock features. Yet this generalisation must be qualified, for there has been an important period of marine erosion since the last ice-sheet disappeared (p. 123).

Sea-level changes in southeast Scotland

Since the most detailed evidence for changes in the relative levels of land and sea in Scotland during and after the disappearance of the last ice-sheet is for southeast Scotland, it is necessary to refer to this evidence first. The basic evidence comprises maps at 1:10,560 scale of glacial, fluvioglacial, marine and estuarine features, about 12,000 accurately-levelled points on raised shorelines and related features, over 2500 boreholes put down by hand, a similar number of commercial borehole records, and a series of radiocarbon dates and pollen analyses.

The oldest lateglacial shorelines identified in southeast Scotland are in East Fife (fig. 9.1). Here each of six shorelines slopes less steeply than its predecessor owing to isostatic tilting during the period of their formation, gradients ranging from 1.26 m/km for the oldest to 0.60 m/km for the youngest. Contemporaneous glacier decay is indicated by the tendency of younger shorelines to extend farther west, ice-margin positions in some instances being recorded by outwash spreads that begin in kame and kettle areas. The shorelines are tilted towards a direction approximately 18° south of east (Cullingford and Smith 1966). From the gradient and age of three later shorelines in southeast Scotland, Andrews and Dugdale (1970) calculated the ages of the East Fife shorelines as ranging from 18,250 to 15,100 B.P. Using more recent data these figures become 17,600 and 14,750. These dates appear inconsistent with evidence that the ice-sheet margin was

situated far to the south in England some 18,000 to 17,000 radiocarbon years ago.

Ice-sheet decay after the formation of the East Fife features
allowed the sea to extend farther west into the firths of Forth and
Tay, some of the contemporary sea-levels being recorded by outwash merging into raised beaches. Ice margin retreat was not
necessarily continuous: for example, the sequence of deposits
revealed by bores at Rosyth dockyard suggests a stillstand or
minor readvance of the ice margin (Sissons and Rhind 1970).

The most pronounced lateglacial raised beach in southeast
Scotland as a whole is the Main Perth, its width often exceeding
200 m. It is related to outwash spreads at its western limit,
merging into them at Larbert in the Carron valley (fig. 9.2) and
between Falkirk and Stirling in the Forth valley (Sissons and
Smith 1965a). Trend-surface analysis of some 500 shoreline
altitudes shows that the shoreline slopes towards E 17°S at an
average gradient of 0.43 m/km (Smith *et al.*, 1969). Subsequent
ice decay was associated for a time with the formation of
further outwash deposits and lower raised beaches, the latter

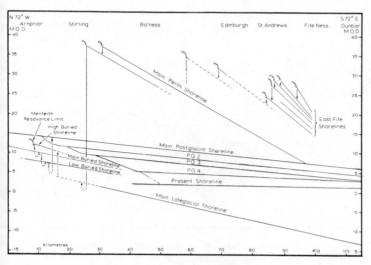

Fig. 9.1   Lateglacial and postglacial shorelines in southeast Scotland,
modified from Sissons, Smith and Cullingford (1966).

being especially clear around the Earn-Tay confluence (Cullingford 1972). In the Forth valley a raised beach slightly below the Main Perth extends up valley towards Stirling where it merges into outwash that in turn merges into kames and kettles. At its western limit the shoreline attains 38 m, but a short distance west of Stirling the highest shorelines do not exceed 20 m (not shown in fig. 9.1 since correlation is uncertain). This pronounced drop in the marine limit suggests a halt in ice retreat or possibly a minor readvance, although the marked constriction in the Forth valley at the Stirling gap may have been a significant factor.

Continued isostatic uplift resulted in a period of low sea-level, during which extensive marine erosion occurred. Around Grangemouth, despite inland location, an area of at least 28 km^2 was

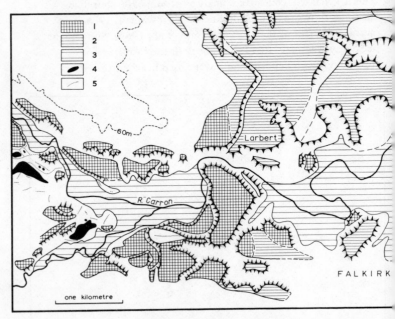

Fig. 9.2   Fluvioglacial forms and raised beaches near Falkirk. 1. Outwash spreads, kame terraces and flattish-topped kames. 2. Lateglacial raised beaches. 3. Floodplains and postglacial terraces (including terraced carse). 4. Kettle holes. 5. Kames.

planated by the sea to produce a gently-sloping layer of gravel
that rests mainly on soft lateglacial marine deposits but also on
planated till and bedrock (fig. 9.3). This gravel layer is now concealed beneath later deposits but its extent and altitude are
known in the Grangemouth area from about 1000 boreholes. The
largest areas of rock and till planation lie close to Ordnance
Datum, while a sharp break of slope terminates the marine
abrasion feature inland in many places at this altitude. This shoreline is referred to as the Main Lateglacial Shoreline. In places the
abrasion platform, cut in soft deposits, continues inland of this
shoreline, but with a steeper gradient. More often the shoreline is

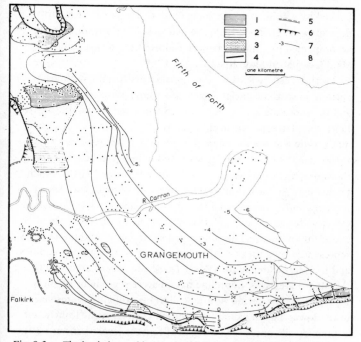

Fig. 9.3   The buried gravel layer around Grangemouth, based on Sissons
(1969). 1. Planated bedrock. 2. Planated till. 3. Bedrock stripped of pre-
existing drift by lateglacial marine erosion. 4. Main Lateglacial Shoreline.
5. Landward edge of carse (shown where other data permit). 6. Steep bluff.
7. Contours on the surface of the buried gravel layer (metres). 8. Boreholes.

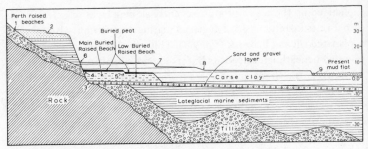

Fig. 9.4   Diagrammatic section showing superficial deposits and
morphology in the mid-Forth valley, modified from Sissons, Smith and
Cullingford (1966).

backed by a zone in which some or all of the pre-existing drift
deposits were stripped from the bedrock. Thus a transgression,
accompanied by limited erosion, followed the formation of the
Main Lateglacial Shoreline (Sissons 1969).

Farther east, at Rosyth, the abrasion platform, cut almost
entirely in soft lateglacial marine sediments, is up to 800 m wide
and the shoreline is at about –4 m (Sissons and Rhind 1970). At
Leith the platform, cut in till (and locally in bedrock), is a kilometre wide and the shoreline is at –5 m. Farther east, at
Cockenzie the platform is at least 300 m broad in bedrock and
the shoreline lies between –9 and –10 m (Sissons 1974b). Much
farther east, at Burnmouth (9 km north of Berwick), undersea
investigations have revealed that marine planation was even more
effective for an abrasion platform cut in bedrock is probably
about 600 m broad. The submerged shoreline, at about –18 m, is
represented by a break of slope and by a belt of rounded cobbles
and boulders (Eden *et al.* 1969). These and other data show that
the Main Lateglacial Shoreline has an average gradient of about
0.17 m/km. The period of low sea-level is probably represented
in the lower Tweed valley for a buried channel, significantly not
containing till, appears to be related to a sea-level of about –20 m
(Rhind 1972).

The period of marine erosion, and the transgression that
accompanied at least the later part of it, ended about the time
the Loch Lomond Readvance reached its greatest extent. A
buried raised beach (High Buried Beach) exists immediately out-

side the Menteith morainic arc and partly overlies outwash
associated with meltwater channels cut into the moraine, but
does not occur within it. Thus glacier ice still stood at the
moraine when the beach was being formed, suggesting an age for
the latter of about 10,300 to 10,100 B.P. Subsequently sea-level
fell to form the Main and Low buried beaches (figs. 9.4 and 9.5),
whose ages are indicated by radiocarbon dates and pollen
analyses to be about 9600 and 8800 B.P. respectively (Sissons
1966; Newey 1966; Kemp 1971; Sissons and Brooks 1971;
Cullingford 1972). The average gradient of the Main Buried
Shoreline in the western part of the Forth valley is 0.146 m/km,
but this figure conceals significant variations, for the shoreline is
horizontal in places and in two localities is dislocated (by 1 m
and 1½ m respectively). These variations (not indicated in fig.
9.1) show that, in this part of the Forth valley at least, isostatic
uplift did not produce the simple tilting of the land that is

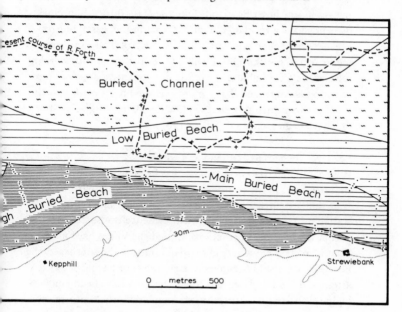

Fig. 9.5 Buried raised beaches beneath the Carse of Stirling between
Kippen and Arnprior. Hand boreholes shown by dots and sections by
crosses.

normally assumed (Brooks 1972; Sissons 1972b).

The intermittent fall of sea-level recorded by the three buried beaches terminated about 8500 B.P. and was succeeded by the major postglacial marine transgression. During the most rapid part of the transgression sea-level at the Menteith moraine, despite isostatic uplift, rose 7 m in a thousand years relative to the land. In the long sheltered inlets of Forth and Tay deposition of estuarine muds occurred to form extensive areas of carse, concealing the now-buried beaches and the peat that had accumulated on them. In two areas, each one to two kilometres across, peat growth kept pace with the accumulation of the muds (Sissons and Smith 1965b). The culmination of the transgression is marked by the Main Postglacial Shoreline, shown by radiocarbon dating to have been abandoned before 6500 B.P. in the western Forth valley (Sissons and Brooks 1971). This shoreline is often a very clear feature and extends for many tens of kilometres in southeast Scotland. Like the Main Buried Shoreline, it does not have a regular gradient (at least in the west), but its average gradient as calculated from about 1000 altitude measurements is 0.076 m/km. Following the formation of this shoreline relative sea-level fell intermittently and extensive deposition of carse muds continued in the more sheltered parts of the Forth valley, where three shorelines below the Main Postglacial Shoreline have been identified (Smith 1968).

Sea-level changes in Scotland as a whole

It is reasonable to expect that sea-level changes similar to those that occurred in the southeast took place in other parts of Scotland similarly located with respect to the probable centre of isostatic uplift. Unfortunately present evidence is insufficient to permit detailed reconstructions. Buried shorelines have not yet been identified anywhere in Scotland outside the southeast (the necessary detailed borehole investigations not having been attempted) and no lateglacial raised beaches have been convincingly reconstructed. Furthermore, much published information on raised shorelines in Scotland is inaccurate and/or misleading, a matter that is not appropriately discussed here.

In areas peripheral to the main area of isostatic uplift a

marked outward descent in the upper limit of marine features is evident. Thus on the Moray Firth coast from the vicinity of Elgin to the Brora area lateglacial raised beaches between 25 m and almost 30 m have been described by various authors (e.g. Ogilvie 1923), yet lateglacial raised beaches are absent or at a very low level in northern Caithness and north-eastern Aberdeenshire. On the west Highland coast in Argyllshire and Inverness-shire raised beaches extend up to altitudes of 30-40 m or even higher (McCann 1964; Peacock 1970), but they are said not to exceed 18 m at Ullapool (Kirk *et al.* 1966) and are absent or at a very low level in the extreme north-west. Similarly, shingle ridges up to 32 m have been reported as occurring in Iona (Synge and Stephens 1966) but in the southern islands of the Outer Hebrides lateglacial marine features appear to be absent. A similar decline in the marine limit occurs from southwest Scotland into north-west England. This widespread outward decline in altitude invites comparison with southeast Scotland where lateglacial shorelines reach 28 m a few kilometres from Fife Ness but have apparently fallen below the altitude of postglacial features by the time Berwick is reached. The outward slope is unlikely to be a syn-chronous shoreline and it probably represents the generalised proximal parts of a series of more steeply-sloping shorelines.

Coasts where the marine limit is much less variable in altitude include Brora-Elgin, much of the west Highland coast southwards from southern Skye (including Mull, Jura and Islay) and the coasts of most of the Firth of Clyde. These areas are comparable with the Forth valley from near Fife Ness to Stirling.

A striking feature of the Forth shoreline sequence is the abrupt fall in the marine limit from 38 m to 20 m at the Stirling gap (p. 122). D.G. Sutherland (unpublished) has suggested that this fall correlates with the similar abrupt (northward) descent of the marine limit he has demonstrated by detailed work in the Loch Fyne/Long area. By southern Loch Fyne the marine limit descends from 36 to 16 m, in Glendaruel from 37 to 15 m or less, and by southern Loch Long from 40 to 14 m. An ice-sheet stillstand or minor readvance is suggested by Sutherland to account for this pattern (although the situation in Loch Long may be complicated by the Loch Lomond Readvance). A stillstand or minor readvance has also been suggested by Peacock (1970) for western Inverness-shire, where raised beaches at 30-40 m (and possibly higher) terminate at the mouths of the sea lochs or some distance within them. It has long been recognised that a marked drop of sea-level accompanied ice-sheet decay in the firths of Beauly, Cromarty and Dornoch on the east coast (e.g. Ogilvie 1923; Read *et al.* 1926). It seems likely that the evidence from these various localities relates to a single event and that this limit of the Highland ice mass broadly reflects the importance of ice-berg calving during ice-sheet decay.

Since the marine limit at Stirling and by the Clyde sea lochs attains 36-40 m, a similar marine limit might be expected in the Glasgow area. Yet it is only 25 m, implying that the Glasgow area was still ice-covered when ice stood at the Stirling/Loch Fyne limit mentioned above. At this time the Firth of Clyde must have been free of glacier ice and, to allow the sea to penetrate into Loch Long, the margin of the ice mass that covered the Glasgow area must have been situated no farther west than Gourock. The implication is that the ice margin retreated *up* the Clyde estuary, contrary to the accepted view (Sissons 1974c). Furthermore, since the marine limit inside the Stirling/Loch Fyne line is 14-20 m, the Glasgow marine limit of 25 m implies deglaciation of the Glasgow area while ice stood at that line. This is turn suggests that the ice at the Stirling/Loch Fyne line was active while that in the Glasgow area was dead.

On parts of the west coast of Scotland, especially on the coasts of the Firth of Lorne, there is a pronounced raised rock platform and cliff that are often cut in resistant metamorphic and igneous rocks. The platform is typically 20-30 m broad but sometimes exceeds 150 m and the cliff is often nearly vertical and over 15 m high. Undercuts, caves, stacks and natural arches are well developed in places. In recent years the features have been interpreted as interglacial despite their optimal development in an area of intense glacial erosion, and possible striae, ice-moulding and till are said to be associated with them (Synge and Stephens 1966; McCann 1966b, 1968; Sissons 1967a; Gray 1974). The evidence that the features have been glaciated is unconvincing, however, and early workers such as E.B. Bailey and W.B. Wright

considered the rock features to be postglacial. Rather does it
appear that they equate with the pronounced lateglacial marine
erosion features of southeast Scotland (Sissons 1974b). The most
detailed study of these raised marine features, by Gray (1974),
shows that the raised shoreline slopes westwards at an average
gradient of 0.16 m/km from the Oban area through eastern Mull,
a gradient that is not uniform however. The period of important
marine erosion demonstrated by the features on both sides of
Scotland is quite exceptional in the history of lateglacial and postglacial marine events and requires special conditions to explain it.
These conditions are provided by the very cold climate of the
Loch Lomond Stadial (and perhaps also the later part of the preceding interstadial) when the erosion of bedrock would be
greatly assisted by semi-diurnal freezing and thawing in the inter-
tidal zone, while the erosion of unconsolidated sediments would
be facilitated by slumping and flowing associated with seasonal
thawing.

At the western end of Loch Shiel, at Corran on Loch Linnhe,
by Loch Creran, at the entrance to Loch Etive, and by Loch Ba
and at the mouth of Glen Forsa in Mull outwash spreads interpreted as formed at or close to the limit of the Loch Lomond
Readvance indicate that sea-level was relatively low when they
accumulated (McCann 1961, 1966a; Peacock 1970; Gray 1972).
The contemporary sea-level has not been determined, however,
owing to modification of the evidence by postglacial seas. In
terms of the interpretation given above these outwash spreads
originally sloped down approximately to the level of the Main
Lateglacial Shoreline.

Periods of low or relatively low sea-level are demonstrated at
many points on the Scottish coasts by buried or submerged peat
beds. The oldest so far dated occur near the head of the Solway
(Redkirk Point), the dates ranging from 10,300±185 to
12,290±250 B.P. Fifteen dates on peat or related material
directly underlying the deposits of the main postglacial transgression in southwest Scotland that vary from 9620±150 to
6800±250 B.P. (e.g. Jardine 1971; Bishop and Dickson 1970) may
be compared with eighteen dates from a similar stratigraphic
position in southeast Scotland that range between 9945±160 and

7480±125 B.P. Unfortunately the southwest Scotland dates are not linked with pollen analyses or with a buried beach sequence so that their significance cannot be fully assessed.

The oldest radiocarbon date for peat resting on postglacial estuarine or marine deposits in southwest Scotland is 6645±120 B.P. from Lochar Moss near Dumfries. Nichols (1967) concluded from bore data and pollen analyses that this peat began to accumulate as the sea receded. Taken in conjunction with the

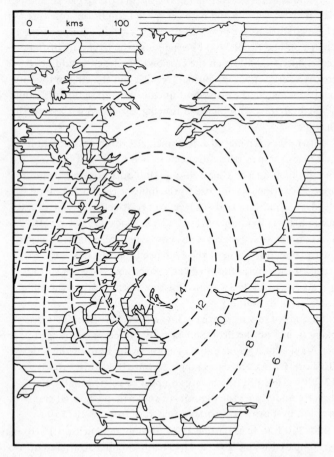

Fig. 9.6   Generalised isobases for the Main Postglacial Raised Shoreline.

youngest date for buried peat from southwest Scotland, it thus appears that the culmination of the major postglacial trans- gression, marked by the Main Postglacial Shoreline, occurred between 6800±250 and 6645±120 B.P. D.Walker (1966) inferred from pollen analyses related to the Scaleby Moss radiocarbon- dated pollen site that the transgression culminated between 6950 and 6600 B.P. on the Cumberland coast. These dates accord with the evidence from the western Forth valley that sea-level there was already falling from its highest postglacial level by 6500 B.P.

The altitude of the Main Postglacial Shoreline is shown by generalised isobases in figure 9.6. Accurate isobases cannot yet be constructed since reliable data are lacking for most of Scotland. The highest known altitude of the shoreline is 15 m at the western end of the Forth valley. In contrast it is very close to Ordnance Datum in mid-Lancashire (Tooley 1974 and unpub- lished) while submerged peat off the coast of Bressay in Shetland dated at 6970±100 and 6670±100 (Hoppe 1965) shows that here the shoreline is more than 9 m below present high-water mark.

The fall of sea-level from the Main Postglacial Shoreline that resulted from continued isostatic uplift in Scotland (excluding peripheral areas such as Shetland, where submergence prevailed) was accompanied by the formation of lower postglacial shore- lines. The only detailed evidence currently available outside the southeast, however, is for the Oban area and eastern Mull. Here Gray (1972) has recognised two fairly definite shorelines below the Main Postglacial and two possible shorelines, but their ages are unknown. Thus in this respect, as with other aspects of the geomorphology of Scotland, a little is known and a vast amount remains to be discovered.

References

AHLMANN, H.W. (1948) Glaciological research on the North Atlantic coasts. *R. Geogr. Soc. Res. Ser.* 1.

ANDERSON, F.W. and DUNHAM, K.C. (1966) The geology of northern Skye. *Mem. Geol. Surv. Scot.*

ANDERSON, J.G.C. (1951) Geology of the Glen Tromie hydro-electric tunnels, Inverness-shire. *Geol. Mag.* 88, 133-9.

ANDREWS, J.T. and DUGDALE, R.E. (1970) Age prediction of glacio-isostatic strandlines based on their gradients. *Bull. Geol. Soc. Am.* 81, 3769-71.

AVERY, O.E., BURTON, G.D. and HEIRTZLER, J.R. (1968) An aeromagnetic survey of the Norwegian Sea. *J. Geophys. Res.* 73, 4583-600.

BAILEY, E.B., *et al.* (1916) The geology of Ben Nevis and Glen Coe. *Mem. Geol. Surv. Scot.*

BAILEY, E.B., *et al.* (1924) Tertiary and post-Tertiary geology of Mull, Loch Aline and Oban. *Mem. Geol. Surv. Scot.*

BALL, D.F. and GOODIER, R. (1974) Ronas Hill, Shetland: a preliminary account of its ground pattern features resulting from the action of frost and wind. In R. Goodier (ed.) *The natural environment of Shetland*, 89-106. Nature Conservancy Council, Edinburgh.

BARROW, G. *et al.* (1912) The geology of the districts of Braemar, Ballater and Glen Clova. *Mem. Geol. Surv. Scot.*

BARROW, G. *et al.* (1913) The geology of upper Strathspey, Gaick and the Forest of Atholl. *Mem. Geol. Surv. Scot.*

BENNIE, J. (1896) On the occurrence of peat with Arctic plants in boulder-clay at Faskine, near Airdrie, Lanarkshire. *Trans. Geol. Soc. Glasg.* 10, 148-52.

BINNS, P.E., McQUILLIN, R. and KENOLTY, N. (1973) The geology of the Sea of the Hebrides. *Inst. Geol. Sci. Rept* 73/14.

BIRKS, H.J.B. (1973) *The past and present vegetation of the Isle of Skye: a palaeoecological study.* Cambridge.

BIRKS, H.J.B. and RANSOM, M.E. (1969) An interglacial peat at Fugla Ness, Shetland. *New Phytol.* 68, 777-96.

BISHOP, W.W. (1963) Lateglacial deposits near Lockerbie, Dumfriesshire. *Trans. J. Proc. Dumfries. Galloway Nat. Hist. Antiq. Soc.* 40, 117-32.

BISHOP, W.W. and DICKSON, J.H. (1970) Radiocarbon dates for the Scottish lateglacial sea in the Firth of Clyde. *Nature* 227, 480-2.

BOTT, M.H.P. (1968) The geological structure of the Irish Sea basin. In D.T. Donovan (ed.), *Geology of shelf seas*, 93-115.

BREMNER, A. (1934) The glaciation of Moray and ice movements in the north of Scotland. *Trans. Edinb. Geol. Soc.* 13, 17-56.

BREMNER, A. (1939) The lateglacial geology of the Tay basin from Pass of Birnam to Grandtully and Pitlochry. *Trans. Edinb. Geol. Soc.* 13, 473-4.

BREMNER, A. (1942) The origin of the Scottish river system. *Scot. Geogr. Mag.* 58, 15-20, 54-9, 99-103.

BROCKS, C.L. (1972) Pollen analysis and the Main Buried Beach in the western part of the Forth valley. *Trans. Inst. Br. Geogr.* 55, 161-70.

BURKE, M.J. (1969) The Forth valley: an ice-moulded lowland. *Trans. Inst. Br. Geogr.* 48, 51-9.

CADELL, H.M. (1886) The Dumbartonshire highlands. *Scot. Geogr. Mag.* 2, 337-47.

CHARLESWORTH, J.K. (1926) The readvance marginal kame-moraine of the south of Scotland and some later stages of retreat. *Trans. R. Soc. Edinb.* 55, 25-50.

CHARLESWORTH, J.K. (1955) Lateglacial history of the Highlands and islands of Scotland. *Trans. R. Soc. Edinb.* 62, 769-928.

CLAPPERTON, C.M. (1970) The evidence for a Cheviot ice-cap. *Trans. Inst. Br. Geogr.* 50, 115-27.

CLAPPERTON, C.M. and SUGDEN, D.E. (1972) The Aberdeen and Dinnet glacial limits reconsidered. In C.M. Clapperton (ed.), *North-East Scotland: geographical essays*, 5-11.

COOPE, G.R. (1962) Coleoptera from a peat interbedded between two boulder clays at Burnhead, near Airdrie. *Trans. Geol. Soc. Glasg.* 24, 279-86.

COOPE, G.R. and BROPHY, J.A. (1972) Lateglacial environmental changes indicated by a coleopteran succession from North Wales. *Boreas*, 1, 97-142.

COOPE, G.R., MORGAN, A. and OSBORNE, P.J. (1971) Fossil Coleoptera as indicators of climatic fluctuations during the last glaciation in Britain. *Palaeogeogr., Palaeoclimatol., Palaeoecol.* 10, 87-101.

CRAMPTON, C.B., *et al.* (1914) The geology of Caithness. *Mem. Geol. Surv. Scot.*

CROFTS, R. (1972) Coastal sediments and processes around St Cyrus. In C.M. Clapperton (ed.), *North-East Scotland: geographical essays*, 15-19.

CULLINGFORD, R.A. (1972) *Lateglacial and postglacial shoreline displacement in the Earn-Tay area and eastern Fife.* Univ. of Edinb. Ph.D. thesis (unpubl.).

CULLINGFORD, R.A. and SMITH, D.E. (1966) Lateglacial shorelines in eastern Fife. *Trans. Inst. Br. Geogr.* 39, 31-51.

DAVIES, G.L. (1956) The parish of North Uist. *Scot. Geogr. Mag.* 72, 65-80.

DONNER, J.J. (1957) The geology and vegetation of lateglacial retreat stages in Scotland. *Trans. R. Soc. Edinb.* 63, 221-64.

EDEN, R.A., ARDUS, D.A., BINNS, P.E., McQUILLIN, R. and WILSON, J.B. (1971) Geological investigations with a manned submersible off the west coast of Scotland 1969-70. *Inst. Geol. Sci. Rept* 71/16.

EDEN, R.A., CARTER, A.V.F. and McKEOWN, M.C. (1969) Submarine examination of lower Carboniferous strata on inshore regions of the continental shelf of southeast Scotland. *Marine Geol.* 7, 235-51.

ESMARK, J. (1827) Remarks tending to explain the geological history of the earth. *Edinb. New Phil. J.* 2, 107-21.

FITZPATRICK, E.A. (1963) Deeply weathered rock in Scotland, its occurrence, age, and contribution to the soils. *J. Soil Sci.* 14, 33-43.

FITZPATRICK, E.A. (1965) An interglacial soil at Teindland, Morayshire. *Nature* 207, 621-2.

FITZPATRICK, E.A. (1972) The principal Tertiary and Pleistocene events in northeast Scotland. In C.M. Clapperton (ed.), *North-East Scotland: geographical essays*, 1-4.

FLEET, H. (1938) Erosion surfaces in the Grampian Highlands of Scotland. *Rapp. Comm. Cartog. des Surfaces d'Appl. Tert., Internat. Geogr. Union*, 91-4.

FLINN, D. (1969a) A geological interpretation of the aeromagnetic maps of the continental shelf around Orkney and Shetland. *Geol. J.* 6, 279-92.

FLINN, D. (1969b) On the development of coastal profiles in the north of Scotland, Orkney and Shetland. *Scot. J. Geol.* 5, 393-9.

FRANCIS, E.H. *et al.* (1970) The geology of the Stirling district. *Mem. Geol. Surv. Scot.*

GEIKIE, A. (1863) On the phenomena of the glacial drift of Scotland. *Trans. Geol. Soc. Glasg.* 1, 1-190.

GEIKIE, A. (1865 (1st ed.), 1901 (3rd ed.)) *The scenery of Scotland.*

GEIKIE, J. (1894) *The great ice age* (3rd ed.).

GEMMELL, A.M.D. (1973) The deglaciation of the island of Arran, Scotland. *Trans. Inst. Br. Geogr.* 59, 25-39.

GEORGE, T.N. (1955) Drainage in the Southern Uplands: Clyde, Nith, Annan. *Trans. Geol. Soc. Glasg.* 22, 1-34.

GEORGE, T.N. (1958) The geology and geomorphology of the Glasgow district. In R. Miller and J. Tivy (eds.), *The Glasgow region*, 17-61.

GEORGE, T.N. (1960) The stratigraphical evolution of the Midland valley. *Trans. Geol. Soc. Glasg.* 24, 32-107.

GEORGE, T.N. (1965) The geological growth of Scotland. In G.Y. Craig (ed.), *The geology of Scotland*, 1-48.

GEORGE, T.N. (1966) Geomorphic evolution in Hebridean Scotland. *Scot. J. Geol.* 2, 1-34.

GODARD, A. (1965) *Recherches de géomorphologie en Ecosse du Nord-ouest.*

GOODLET, G.A. (1964) The kamiform deposits near Carstairs, Lanark-shire. *Bull. Geol. Surv. Gt Brit.* 21, 175-96.

GRAY, J.M. (1972) *The inter-, late- and post-glacial shorelines, and ice-limits of Lorn and eastern Mull.* Univ. of Edinb. Ph.D. thesis (unpubl.).

GRAY, J.M. (1974) The main rock platform of the Firth of Lorn, western Scotland. *Trans. Inst. Br. Geogr.* 61, 81-99.

GRAY, J.M. and BROOKS, C.L. (1972) The Loch Lomond Readvance moraines of Mull and Menteith. *Scot. J. Geol.* 8, 95-103.

GREGORY, J.W. (1913) *The nature and origin of fjords.*

HALL, J. (1815) On the revolutions of the earth's surface. *Trans. R. Soc. Edinb.* 7, 139-211.

HAYNES, V.M. (1968) The influence of glacial erosion and rock structure on corries in Scotland. *Geogr. Ann.* 50A, 221-34.

HOLGATE, N. (1969) Palaeozoic and Tertiary transcurrent movements on the Great Glen fault. *Scot. J. Geol.* 5, 97-139.

HOLLINGWORTH, S.E. (1938) The recognition and correlation of high-level erosion surfaces in Britain: a statistical study. *Quart. J. Geol. Soc.* 94, 55-84.

HOPPE, G. (1965) Submarine peat in the Shetland Islands. *Geogr. Ann.* 47a, 195-203.

JAMIESON, T.F. (1863) On the parallel roads of Glen Roy, and their place in the history of the glacial period. *Quart. J. Geol. Soc.* 19, 235-59.

JAMIESON, T.F. (1865) On the history of the last geological changes in Scotland. *Quart. J. Geol. Soc.* 21, 161-203.

JARDINE, W.G. (1959) River development in Galloway. *Scot. Geogr. Mag.* 75, 65-74.

JARDINE, W.G. (1966) Landscape evolution in Galloway. *Trans. J. Proc. Dumfries. Galloway Nat. Hist. Antiq. Soc.* 43, 1-13.

JARDINE, W.G. (1971) Form and age of late Quaternary shorelines and coastal deposits of south-west Scotland: critical data. *Quaternaria* 14, 103-14.

KEMP, D.D. (1971) *The stratigraphy and sub-carse morphology of an area on the northern side of the river Forth, between the Lake of Menteith and Kincardine-on-Forth.* Univ. of Edinb. Ph.D. thesis (unpubl.).

KENNEDY, W.Q. (1946) The Great Glen fault. *Quart. J. Geol. Soc.* 102, 41-72.

KING, R.B. (1971a) Boulder polygons and stripes in the Cairngorm Mountains, Scotland. *J. Glaciol.* 10, 375-86.

KING, R.B. (1971b) Vegetation destruction in the sub-Alpine zones of the Cairngorm Mountains. *Scot. Geogr. Mag.* 87, 103-15.

KIRBY, R.P. (1968) The ground moraines of Midlothian and East Lothian. *Scot. J. Geol.* 4, 209-20.

KIRBY, R.P. (1969a) Morphometric analysis of glaciofluvial terraces in the Esk basin, Midlothian. *Trans. Inst. Br. Geogr.* 48, 1-18.

KIRBY, R.P. (1969b) Till fabric analyses from the Lothians, central Scotland. *Geogr. Ann.* 51A, 48-60.

KIRK, W. and GODWIN, H. (1963) A lateglacial site at Loch Droma, Ross and Cromarty. *Trans. R. Soc. Edinb.* 65, 225-49.

KIRK, W., RICE, R.J. and SYNGE, F.M. (1966) Deglaciation and vertical displacement of shorelines in Wester and Easter Ross. *Trans. Inst. Br. Geogr.* 39, 65-78.

LINTON, D.L. (1933) The origin of the Tweed drainage system. *Scot. Geogr. Mag.* 49, 162-75.

LINTON, D.L. (1949) Some Scottish river captures re-examined. *Scot. Geogr. Mag.* 65, 123-32.

LINTON, D.L. (1951a) Problems of Scottish scenery. *Scot. Geogr. Mag.* 67, 65-85.

LINTON, D.L. (1951b) Watershed breaching by ice in Scotland. *Trans. Inst. Br. Geogr.* 15, 1-15.

LINTON, D.L. (1954) Some Scottish river captures re-examined. III. The beheading of the Don. *Scot. Geogr. Mag.* 70, 64-78.

LINTON, D.L. (1955) The problem of tors. *Geogr. J.* 121, 470-87.

LINTON, D.L. (1957) Radiating valleys in glaciated lands. *Tijds. van bet Koninklijk Nederlandsch Aardrijkskundig Genootschap* 74, 297-312.

LINTON, D.L. (1959) Morphological contrasts between eastern and western Scotland. In R. Miller and J.W. Watson (eds.) *Geographical essays in memory of Alan G. Ogilvie,* 16-45.

LINTON, D.L. (1962) Glacial erosion on soft-rock outcrops in central Scotland. *Biul Peryglac.* 11, 247-57.

LINTON, D.L. (1963) The forms of glacial erosion. *Trans. Inst. Br. Geogr.* 33, 1-28.

LINTON, D.L. and MOISLEY, H.A. (1960) The origin of Loch Lomond. *Scot. Geogr. Mag.* 76, 26-37.

LUMSDEN, G.I. and DAVIES, A. (1965) The buried channel of the river Nith and its marked change in level across the Southern Upland fault. *Scot. J. Geol.* 1, 134-43.

MACKINDER, J.H. (1902) The snowline in Britain. *Geogr. Ann.* 31, 179-93 197-93

MANLEY, G. (1952) *Climate and the British scene.*

MANLEY, G. (1964) The evolution of the climatic environment. In J.W. Watson and J.B. Sissons (eds.), *The British Isles: a systematic geography,* 152-70.

MATHIESON, J., and BAILEY, E.B. (1925) The glacial strand-lines of Loch Tulla. *Trans. Edinb. Geol. Soc.* 11, 193-9.

McCANN, S.B. (1961) Some supposed 'raised beach' deposits at Corran, Loch Linnhe, and Loch Etive. *Geol. Mag.* 98, 131-42.

McCANN, S.B. (1964) The raised beaches of northeast Islay and western Jura, Argyll. *Trans. Inst. Br. Geogr.* 35, 1-16.

McCANN, S.B. (1966a) The limits of the Lateglacial Highland, or Loch Lomond, Readvance along the west Highland seaboard from Oban to Mallaig. *Scot. J. Geol.* 2, 84-95

McCANN, S.B. (1966b) The Main Postglacial Raised Shoreline of western Scotland from the Firth of Lorne to Loch Broom. *Trans. Inst. Br. Geogr.* 39, 87-99.

McCANN, S.B. (1968) Raised rock platforms in the western isles of Scotland. In E.G. Bowen, H. Carter and J.A. Taylor (eds.) *Geography at Aberystwyth,* 22-34. London.

McCANN, S.B. and RICHARDS, A. (1969) The coastal features of the island of Rhum in the Inner Hebrides. *Scot. J. Geol.* 5, 15-25.

McLELLAN, A.G. (1969) The last glaciation and deglaciation of central Lanarkshire. *Scot. J. Geol.* 5, 248-68.

McMANUS, J. (1966) An ice-wedge and associated phenomena in the Lower Limestone Series of Fife. *Scot. J. Geol.* 2, 259-64.

McMANUS, J. (1967) Preglacial diversion of the Tay drainage through the Perth gap. *Scot. Geogr. Mag.* 83, 138-9.

MILLER, R., COMMON, R., and GALLOWAY, R.W. (1954) Stone stripes and other surface features of Tinto Hill. *Geogr. J.* 120, 216-19.

MITCHELL, G.F., PENNY, L.F., SHOTTON, F.W. and WEST, R.G. (1973) A correlation of Quaternary deposits in the British Isles. Geol. Soc. London. Special Report 4.

MOAR, N.T. (1969) Late Weichselian and Flandrian pollen diagrams from southwest Scotland. *New Phytol.* 68, 433-67.

MORT, F.W. (1918) The rivers of southwest Scotland. *Scot. Geogr. Mag.* 34, 361-8.

MURRAY, J., and PULLAR, L. (1910) *Bathymetrical survey of the Scottish freshwater lochs.* 6 vols.

NEWEY, W.W. (1966) Pollen analysis of sub-carse peats of the Forth valley. *Trans. Inst. Br. Geogr.* 39, 53-9.

NEWEY, W.W. (1970) Pollen analysis of Late-Weichselian deposits at Corstorphine, Edinburgh. *New Phytol.* 69, 1167-77.

NICHOLS, H. (1967) Vegetational change, shoreline displacement and the human factor in the late Quaternary history of southwest Scotland. *Trans. R. Soc. Edinb.* 67, 145-87.

OGILVIE, A.G. (1923) The physiography of the Moray Firth coast. *Trans. R. Soc. Edinb.* 53, 377-404.

PAGE.N.R.(1972) On the age of the Hoxnian Interglacial. *Geol. J.*8,129-42.

PATERSON, I.B. (1974) The supposed Perth Readvance in the Perth district. *Scot. J. Geol.* 10, 53-66.

PEACH, B.N. and HORNE, J. (1910) The Scottish lakes in relation to the geological features of the country. In J. Murray and L. Pullar (eds.) *Bathymetrical survey of the Scottish freshwater lochs,* 439-513.

PEACH, B.N. and HORNE, J. (1930) *Chapters in the geology of Scotland.*

PEACH, B.N. *et al.* (1909) The geology of the seaboard of Mid-Argyll. *Mem. Geol. Surv. Scot.*

PEACH, B.N. *et al.* (1913a) The geology of central Ross-shire. *Mem. Geol. Surv. Scot.*

PEACH, B.N. *et al.* (1913b) The geology of the Fannich Mountains and the country around upper Loch Maree and Strath Broom. *Mem. Geol. Surv. Scot.*

PEACOCK, J.D. (1970) Some aspects of the glacial geology of west Inverness-shire. *Bull. Geol. Surv. Great Brit.* 33, 43-56.

PEACOCK, J.D. (1971) Marine shell radiocarbon dates and the chronology of deglaciation in western Scotland. *Nature Phys. Sci.* 230, 43-5.

PEACOCK, J.D., *et al.* (1968) The geology of the Elgin district. *Mem. Geol. Surv. Scot.*

PENNINGTON, W., HAWORTH, E.Y., BONNY, A.P. and LISHMAN, J.P. (1972) Lake sediments in northern Scotland. *Phil. Trans. R. Soc. Lond.* 264B, 191-294.

PÉWÉ, T.L. (1966) Palaeoclimatic significance of fossil ice wedges. *Biul. Peryglac.* 15, 65-73.

PHEMISTER, T.C., and SIMPSON, S. (1949) Pleistocene deep weathering in northeast Scotland. *Nature* 164, 318-19.

PRICE, R.J. (1960) Glacial meltwater channels in the upper Tweed drainage basin. *Geogr. J.* 126, 483-9.

RAGG, J.M. and BIBBY, J.S. (1966) Frost weathering and solifluction products in southern Scotland. *Geogr. Ann.* 48, 12-23.

RAMSAY, A.C. (1878) The *physical geology and geography of Great Britain* (5th ed.).

READ, H.H. (1923) The geology of the country around Banff, Huntly and Turriff. *Mem. Geol. Surv. Scot.*

READ, H.H., *et al.* (1926) The geology of Strath Oykell and lower Loch Shin. *Mem. Geol. Surv. Scot.*

RHIND, D.W. (1969) *The terraces of the Tweed valley.* Univ. of Edinb. Ph.D. thesis (unpubl.).

RHIND, D.W. (1972) The buried valley of the lower Tweed. *Trans. Nat. Hist. Soc. Northumb., Durham, Newcastle upon Tyne* 4, 159-64.

RICHARDS, A. (1969) Some aspects of the evolution of the coastline of northeast Skye. *Scot. Geogr. Mag.* 85, 122-31.

ROBINSON, G., PETERSON, J.A. and ANDERSON, P.M. (1971) Trend surface analysis of corrie altitudes in Scotland. *Scot. Geogr. Mag.* 87, 142-6.

ROLFE, W.D.I. (1966) Woolly rhinoceros from the Scottish Pleistocene. *Scot. J. Geol.* 2, 253-8.

ROMANS, J.C.C., STEVENS, J.H., and ROBERTSON, L. (1966) Alpine soils of northeast Scotland. *J. Soil Sci.* 17, 184-99.

RUDDIMAN, W.F. and McINTYRE, A. (1973) Time-transgressive deglacial retreat of polar waters from the North Atlantic. *Quat. Res.* 3, 117-30.

RYDER, R.H. (1968) *Geomorphological mapping of the Isle of Rhum, Inverness-shire.* Univ. of Glasg. M.Sc. thesis (unpubl.).

RYDER, R.H., and McCANN, S.B. (1971) Periglacial phenomena on the island of Rhum in the Inner Hebrides. *Scot. J. Geol.* 7, 293-303.

SHOTTON, F.W., BLUNDELL, P.J., and WILLIAMS, R.E.G. (1970) Birmingham University radiocarbon dates IV. *Radiocarbon* 12, 385-99.

SIMPSON, J.B. (1933) The late-glacial readvance moraines of the Highland border west of the river Tay. *Trans. R. Soc. Edinb.* 57, 633-45.

SIMPSON, S. (1948) The glacial deposits of Tullos and the Bay of Nigg, Aberdeen. *Trans. R. Soc. Edinb.* 61, 687-98.

SIMPSON, S. (1955) A re-interpretation of the drifts of northeast Scotland. *Trans. Edinb. Geol. Soc.* 16, 189-99.

SISSONS, J.B. (1958) Supposed ice-dammed lakes in Britain with particular reference to the Eddleston valley, southern Scotland. *Geogr. Ann.* 40, 159-87.

SISSONS, J.B. (1960) Erosion surfaces, cyclic slopes and drainage systems in southern Scotland and northern England. *Trans. Inst. Br. Geogr.* 28, 23-38.

SISSONS, J.B. (1966) Relative sea-level changes between 10,300 and 8300 B.P. in part of the Carse of Stirling. *Trans. Inst. Br. Geogr.* 39, 19-29.

SISSONS, J.B. (1967a) *The evolution of Scotland's scenery.* Edinburgh.

SISSONS, J.B. (1967b) Glacial stages and radiocarbon dates in Scotland. *Scot. J. Geol.* 3, 375-81.

SISSONS, J.B. (1969) Drift stratigraphy and buried morphological features in the Grangemouth-Falkirk-Airth area, central Scotland. *Trans. Inst. Br. Geogr.* 48, 19-50.

SISSONS, J.B. (1971) The geomorphology of central Edinburgh. *Scot. Geogr. Mag.* 87, 185-96.

SISSONS, J.B. (1972a) The last glaciers in part of the south-east Grampians. *Scot. Geogr. Mag.* 88, 168-81.

SISSONS, J.B. (1972b) Dislocation and non-uniform uplift of raised shore-lines in the western part of the Forth valley. *Trans. Inst. Br. Geogr.* 55, 145-59.

SISSONS, J.B. (1974a) A lateglacial ice-cap in the central Grampians, Scotland. *Trans. Inst. Br. Geogr.* 62, 95-114.

SISSONS, J.B. (1974b) Lateglacial marine erosion in Scotland. *Boreas,* 3, 41-8.

SISSONS, J.B. (1974c) The Quaternary in Scotland: a review. *Scot. J. Geol.* 10, 34-37.

SISSONS, J.B. and BROOKS, C.L. (1971) Dating of early postglacial land and sea level changes in the western Forth valley. *Nature Phys. Sci.* 234, 124-7.

SISSONS, J.B. and GRANT, A.J.H. (1972) The last glaciers in the Lochnagar area, Aberdeenshire. *Scot. J. Geol.* 8, 85-93.

SISSONS, J.B. and RHIND, D.W. (1970) Drift stratigraphy and buried morphology beneath the Forth at Rosyth. *Scot. J. Geol.* 6, 272-84.

SISSONS, J.B. and SMITH, D.E. (1965a) Raised shorelines associated with the Perth Readvance in the Forth valley and their relation to glacial isostasy. *Trans. R. Soc. Edinb.* 66, 143-68.

SISSONS, J.B. and SMITH, D.E. (1965b) Peat-bogs in a postglacial sea and a buried raised beach in the western part of the Carse of Stirling. *Scot. J. Geol.* 1, 247-55.

SISSONS, J.B., SMITH, D.E. and CULLINGFORD, R.A. (1966) Lateglacial and postglacial shorelines in southeast Scotland. *Trans. Inst. Br. Geogr.* 39, 9-18.

SISSONS, J.B. and WALKER, M.J.C. (1974) Lateglacial site in the central Grampian Highlands. *Nature* 249, 822-4.

SMITH, D.E. (1968) Postglacial displaced shorelines in the surface of the carse clay on the north bank of the river Forth, in Scotland. *Zeits. für Geomorph.* 12, 388-408.

SMITH, D.E., SISSONS, J.B., and CULLINGFORD, R.A. (1969) Isobases for the Main Perth Raised Shoreline in southeast Scotland as determined by trend-surface analysis. *Trans. Inst. Br. Geogr.* 46, 45-52.

SMITH, D.E., THOMPSON, K.S.R. and KEMP, D.D. (in press) The lateglacial and postglacial history of the Teith valley.

SOONS, J.M. (1958) Landscape evolution in the Ochil Hills. *Scot. Geogr. Mag.* 74, 86-97.

SOONS, J.M. (1960) The sub-drift surface of the lower Devon valley. *Trans. Geol. Soc. Glasg.* 24, 1-7.

SUGDEN, D.E. (1968) The selectivity of glacial erosion in the Cairngorm Mountains. *Trans. Inst. Br. Geogr.* 45, 79-92.

SUGDEN, D.E. (1969) The age and form of corries in the Cairngorms. *Scot. Geogr. Mag.* 85, 34-46.

SUGDEN, D.E. (1970) Landforms of deglaciation in the Cairngorm Mountains. *Trans. Inst. Br. Geogr.* 51, 201-19.

SUGDEN, D.E. (1971) The significance of periglacial activity on some Scottish mountains. *Geogr. J.* 137, 388-92.

SYNGE, F.M. (1956) The glaciation of northeast Scotland. *Scot. Geogr. Mag.* 72, 129-43.

SYNGE, F.M. (1963) The Quaternary succession round Aberdeen, North-East Scotland. *Rept. VIth Internat. Quat. Cong., Geomorph. Sect.* 3, 353-61.

SYNGE, F.M., and STEPHENS, N. (1966) Late- and postglacial shorelines, and ice limits in Argyll and northeast Ulster. *Trans. Inst. Br. Geogr.* 39, 101-25.

TOMPSON, H.R. (1950) Some corries of northwest Sutherland. *Proc. Geol. Ass.* 61, 145-55.

THOMPSON, K.S.R. (1972) *The last glaciers in western Perthshire.* Univ. of Edinb. Ph.D. thesis (unpubl.).

TING, S. (1937) The coastal configuration of western Scotland. *Geogr. Ann.* 19, 62-83.

TOOLEY, M.J. (1974) Sea-level changes during the last 9000 years in northwest England. *Geogr. J.* 140, 18-42.

TULLOCH, W., and WALTON, H.S. (1958) The geology of the Midlothian coalfield. *Mem. Geol. Surv. Scot.*

WALKER, D. (1966) The Late Quaternary history of the Cumberland lowland. *Phil. Trans. R. Soc. Lond.* 251B, 1-210.

WALTON, K. (1959) Ancient elements in the coastline of North-East Scotland. In R. Miller and J.W. Watson (eds.) *Geographical essays in memory of Alan G. Ogilvie,* 93-109.

WALTON, K. (1963) Geomorphology. In A.C. O'Dell and J. Mackintosh (eds.), *The North-East of Scotland,* 16-31.

WATTS, A.B. (1971) Geophysical investigations on the continental shelf and slope north of Scotland. *Scot. J. Geol.* 7, 189-218.

von WEYMARN, J., and EDWARDS, K.J. (1973) Interstadial site on the Island of Lewis, Scotland. *Nature* 246, 473-4.

WHITE, I.D. and MOTTERSHEAD, D.N. (1972) Past and present vegetation in relation to solifluction on Ben Arkle, Sutherland. *Trans. Bot. Soc. Edinb.* 41, 475-89.

WRIGHT, J. (1896) Boulder-clay, a marine deposit. *Trans. Geol. Soc. Glasg.* 10, 263-72.

WRIGHT, W.B. (1911) On a pre-glacial shoreline in the western isles of Scotland. *Geol. Mag.* 48, 97-109.

YOUNG, J.A.T. (1974) Ice wastage in Glenmore, upper Spey valley, Inverness-shire. *Scot. J. Geol.*

YOUNG, J.A.T. (in press) Ice wastage in Glen Feshie, Inverness-shire.

Index